The complete illustrated
autobiography of Australia's
greatest ever fast bowler

Dennis
Lillee

AFFIRM
press

Published by Affirm Press in 2017
28 Thistlethwaite Street, South Melbourne, VIC 3205.
www.affirmpress.com.au

10 9 8 7 6 5 4 3 2 1

National Library of Australia Cataloguing-in-Publication entry available for
this title at www.nla.gov.au

Title: Dennis Lillee / Dennis Lillee, author.
ISBN: 9781925584202 (paperback)

Cover and book design by Karen Wallis
Cover image by Patrick Eagar/Patrick Eagar Collection via Getty Images
Printed in China by C&C Printing

The complete illustrated
autobiography of Australia's
greatest ever fast bowler

Dennis
Lillee

I would like to dedicate this book to the memory of my late brother, Trevor. He was a huge part of my journey, which began with our mutual love of cricket and playing 'backyard Tests' with our sister, Carmen.

CONTENTS

THE NIGHT OF MY RETIREMENT FROM TEST CRICKET, AFTER WE'D JUST beaten Pakistan at the SCG, I was wandering into a hotel to catch up with my teammates when I felt a tap on my shoulder. 'Excuse me, didn't you used to be Dennis Lillee?'

It was Geoff Lawson, one of the new brigade. I laughed, but it's a question that has occurred to me more than once since. I loved playing cricket, and a good chunk of my life was taken up either dreaming about playing, training to play or actually playing. But when that was over, I kind of retreated back into a bubble of home life and other business interests that got me fired up. I've never had much interest in being part of the cricket circuit and, as time has passed, I've often felt like my playing days were another lifetime.

Whenever I meet cricket fans, they are always keen to relive moments they remember from my playing career, and I'm reminded of things that I haven't thought about in years. It's like I look back on them the same way the fans do, as if we are talking about somebody else. And I have to admit, I get a thoroughly unexpected boost from it every time. Just like I have putting this book together, thinking to myself, 'Did I really used to be Dennis Lillee? Wow! How lucky was I?!' ●

The significant balls and bails on this spread are part of the collection at the WACA Museum, of which I am proud patron. I haven't kept much personal memorabilia myself, although I couldn't part with the gloves I wore for my highest Test score (top right) or my old shoes (right) showing the innovative hole I cut to keep the integrity of the shoe while giving my toe some relief from all that full-pelt running in.

Cricket Ball
Australia vs England
28,29,30 Aug, 1,2,3, Sept. 1975
Kennington Oval, Kennington

I don't remember much about my maternal grandmother because she died when I was very young, but Len 'Pop' Halifax was a huge influence. It was Len who really instilled in me the importance of fitness. He was a Cockney through and through, and while I was delighted that he got to see me play for Australia, he made no bones about the fact that when we played England he was cheering against me!

— 1 —

LILLEE HERITAGE

I'm immensely proud of my West Australian heritage, so it seems ironic that the greatest influence on my cricketing life was a Pom who cheered against me when my team was playing England.

HAPPY TO BE 'PLAYING'

IF THOSE CLOSEST TO ME IN 1951 COULD HAVE wound the clocks forward and seen me in 1971, they'd have found it impossible to believe I was the same person. I was born on 18 July 1949 in the Perth suburb of Subiaco, and as a toddler it became clear that I had a problem with my ankles and legs, because I would quite regularly fall over when I tried to run.

Mum and Dad were so concerned about my clumsiness that I was made to wear leg braces to keep me on an even keel. The problem persisted for some time, and I developed an uneven gait (aka 'a funny walk').

At that stage my parents would have been delighted if I just got to play sport like other kids and nothing more. If you'd told them that 20 years later I'd be opening the bowling for Australia, they would probably have thought you had rocks in your head. What a transformation!

My dad, Keith, was around 23 and mum, Shirley, 20 when I was born. My brother, Trevor, followed 15 months later and my sister, Carmen, a couple of years after that.

Dad was a long-distance truck driver who mostly worked on unsealed roads in the north of Western Australia. There were times when his road train got stuck in the wet, which meant he was often away for weeks at a time. Mum and Carmen did the household chores while Trevor and I seemed to be forever cutting firewood in the bush, which Dad would collect when he got home.

Whenever we got the chance, Trevor and I, plus as many neighbourhood kids as we could round up, were always looking to play 'Tests' on our front lawn. We used a tennis ball to keep injury and the glazier at bay. Carmen played too but she was only allowed to field; what an arm she developed! She went on to be a very good netball player in underage competitions.

Sometimes we would invade the yard next door and scrape out a pitch. Since it had a very sandy surface, we would place an ancient mattress at the bowling end to make sure we had a reasonable footing on delivery – which resulted in my good balance on delivery as an adult.

TOP LEFT: My paternal grandfather moved over from Kent in England and married in Jarrahdale in 1912. He had the night-cart contract, which would not have been easy – but neither was feeding ten kids. Every Friday after doing his last run he'd hit the pub and drink until closing time. Then he'd slump onto the back of the cart, slap the horse, and it would take him home.

TOP RIGHT: Mum and Dad's wedding day – a striking couple.

BOTTOM: Dad with the wood-carting truck. He was a big, gentle man with huge arms and hands. I remember him downing large trees with an old handsaw, and now he feels like a not-too-distant link to the original pioneers.

That's me, second row, second from the left in my class photo at Belmay Primary School circa 1955. It was a happy time, especially as sport was a high priority for the headmaster, Clive Elliott, who was a very good sportsman himself. One of the teachers, Ken Waters, was a major inspiration for my love of sport.

Me on the left with my sister, Carmen, and late brother, Trevor. We had an idyllic childhood together.

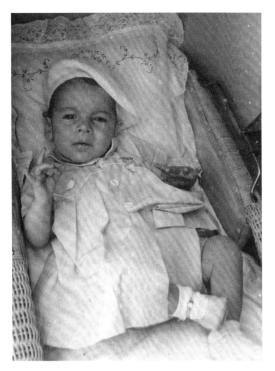

The first and last time I wore a beret.

This cured me of cardigans! Shirt and jumper for me nowadays.

From the outset Trevor, who was always highly competitive, was a better sportsman than me – mainly because he was more coordinated. He was predominantly an opening batsman with tremendous defence, but could also send down a mean leg spinner and could bowl at medium pace with plenty of swing.

I went to Belmay Primary School in the eastern suburbs of Perth and was academically 'average', but I was always top of the class when the bell rang and we rushed out the door to play whatever games were on offer. Cricket, football, athletics, swimming: they all appealed to me back then.

But while my grades weren't too flash, a teacher called Ken Waters sowed in me the seeds of a future in sport. He taught me the fundamentals of several games, but more importantly he instilled in me a will to win.

Dad's knowledge of cricket was pretty sketchy but he was keen to join our Tests. Football was his real passion, and he was a very handy player at ruck forward.

It was my mother's father, Len Halifax, who had the biggest influence on me. 'Pop' had a background in boxing and coached some very good state amateur fighters, but he steered Trevor and me away from the Queensbury rules, saying it was 'a mug's game'.

Whenever Trevor and I went around to Pop's place he would produce a bat and ball, invariably followed by a valuable chat on various aspects of the game and life in general. Pop was always very insistent on fitness, drumming in right from the beginning just how valuable it was in any sport to have a second wind. I'd say Pop was my greatest inspiration when it came to cricket, and I'm delighted that he got to witness most of my Test career. ●

— 2 —

THE YOUNG CRICKETER

I was a 'sensible' teen in many ways and didn't make
too much trouble for my parents. But it was the
opposite when it came to cricket: I was determined,
wild and a bit of a tearaway.

HARD YARDS

I **PLAYED CRICKET ALL MY LIFE, BUT A STINKING-HOT DAY** in Perth marked the true start of my 'cricket career'. It was one of those days when all sensible people headed for their air conditioning or swimming pools, but those luxuries didn't interest me in the slightest (and we didn't possess either anyway).

All I kept thinking was, what if I had to bowl fast for a prolonged spell in the same heat at the WACA? So, when the mercury hit the heights, I pulled on my joggers and hit the scorching pavement. The energy-sapping heat didn't bother me, and I treated it like an opportunity to get fit for any conditions.

I was only at the colts level at that stage. I felt I was making good progress with my bowling, but I knew that to keep on progressing I would have to put in the hard yards. And so I set off from my home in the Perth suburb of Carlisle, stopwatch at the ready, to challenge myself and the elements. Whenever I took to the pavement it was a full-on run, not a jog, so that when I really had to put in on the field it would not be a surprise to my system.

I had always been obsessed by the methods of eccentric athletics coach Percy Cerutty and the performances of his track star, middle-distance runner Herb Elliott. Cerutty used to force Elliott to run up and down sand hills as a method of improving Elliott's stamina. He figured that if Elliott could run in sand, how much easier would it be for him to run a race at a stadium? He was right, and at the 1960 Rome Olympics Elliott won the 1500m by the largest margin ever recorded in the Games' history. Over the six years that Cerutty trained Elliott (from 1956 until 1962), he was the undefeated champion of both the 1500m and the mile.

> I dreamed of scaling the same heights as Herb Elliott, and I firmly believed that running good, very regimented times in extreme heat around suburban streets would give me an edge.

After club practice I would always do extra laps at Lathlain Park or Fletcher Park when the rest of the Perth team packed up and went home. Officials soon got sick of waiting for me to finish and gave me a key so I could lock up the dressing room myself.

As my career entered the Sheffield Shield stage, if our team batted first I would often go for a mid-length run rather than sit there watching the top order doing their stuff. It wasn't rocket science, but I worked out at a very early age that if you merely wanted to play for your club or state you could put in minimal effort. But if you aspired to being better than the competition, you had to put in the extra work to gain an advantage over your opponents and rivals.

This is probably one of my favourite action shots: although not in a game, it shows the effort and power necessary to send a thunderbolt of around 160kph towards a batsman. All those runs in the sweltering heat of Perth when I was a teenager were building towards this.

My parents encouraged me to join the bank as it was seen to offer job security in those days.

GETTING A JOB

I ONCE JUMPED THE FENCE AT THE WACA TO watch the big West Indian speedster Wes Hall. He was my inspiration before I even became a teenager, and I was almost struck dumb by his awesome approach to the wicket and the way he could make the ball fly so fast.

I went to Belmont Senior High School, but by the time I was 15 my interest in school was waning while my passion for cricket was running hot. One of the reasons I didn't like Belmont High was that because it was so new there was little organised sport – and no cricket team. That meant I had no pathway to the junior state teams.

But Belmont High did have a big field and practice nets and, fortunately, a teacher by the name of Dr Frank Pyke. He was a big influence on me, and over the years he became a great friend. He later played a major role in my return to cricket after a back injury.

> I applied for a job at a bank, naively as it turned out, because I thought it would leave me with more time to concentrate on cricket.

I figured that if banks didn't open until 10am and closed at 3.30pm, I could both sleep in and leave work early enough to allow me plenty of time in the nets. It was a good idea

in theory, but some nights I was still stuck in the bank until 7pm trying to balance the till.

Although I was determined to make it as a cricketer, I realised that an actual career in cricket was still a wild dream. All of the top Australian players at the time had to have regular jobs too. So I took my job very seriously and envisaged that one day I would rise to become the manager of a Commonwealth Bank somewhere.

Around the same time I joined the South Belmont Club, where the coach, Mick Basile, took me under his wing. I got to play for the club's junior team on Saturday mornings and one of the lower senior sides in the afternoon. It soon got to the stage where Mick could see me going no further with South Belmont and advised me to join the district team at Perth Cricket Club.

When I was 16 I got to play second grade until almost the end of the summer. I got a call up to first grade, but I took only one wicket in my first game and very few for the rest of the season. I was bowling pretty fast but I was very inaccurate on the slow Lathlain Park wicket, which was probably making me try too hard.

I met Peter Loader, the former England Test fast bowler, who had come to live in Western Australia and was helping to develop fast bowlers at the WACA. Critically, he made sure I was chosen in the state colts

I loved footy but didn't go on with it. Cricket became the all-consuming sport for me (I'm first on the left).

squad with the best young cricketers in Western Australia.

Another major influence at Perth was the captain, Kevin Taylforth, a man who was pretty handy with a ball. He taught me a lot about fast bowling, and he embedded in me two indelible traits: a will to win and a hatred of batsmen.

I was 17 when I went away with the state colts team, and our first game was against Victoria, which had Max Walker and Alan 'Froggy' Thomson opening the bowling. We had a pretty good team, and the best I could

manage was being named 12th man. Stan Wilson, one of the fastest bowlers I ever saw in grade cricket, led the pace attack in a team that also included Rod Marsh, Bob Massie and Terry Gale, the golfer.

Our second game was in Adelaide, and I was called into the side at the last minute when someone pulled out injured. I managed to take wickets in that game, and I dared to dream that I was finally on my way up the ladder. ●

Always asking questions

Dennis was a very serious young man, in cricket and in life. He and his brother, Trevor, came down to South Belmont Cricket Club when I was coaching the under-16s. I used to play football with their dad, Keith, who was a very good centre-forward and ruck. His boys had talent, but the big difference between them was that Trevor was as lazy as Dennis was driven. You'd ask Dennis if he'd run his four laps at training and he'd say, 'No, I've done ten.'

I reckon he was the first person to really put elite fitness into cricket, and it stood him in amazingly good stead. I could bowl fast for 10 overs but never come back at the same speed; Dennis could, again and again.

I was probably the first person to see what Dennis might become. There was this kid, Wally Edwards (who went on to become vice-president and chairman of the WACA and Cricket Australia respectively), who hit three or four centuries on the way to facing us in a final, and Dennis knocked him over in the teens. That was a statement.

I was a fast bowler myself, so I worked a lot with Dennis. He was the sort of young bloke who always asked questions, and I was happy to give him the answers. Even at age 15 he was very methodical and analytical in his approach to bowling. I'd tell him to do something, and he'd ask, 'Why?' He wasn't being cheeky, just keen to understand.

I probably helped him get his feet and brain working together better, but even at that stage he had the technique. I helped toughen him up a bit. I remember saying, 'If a batsman hits you for six, he's not going to apologise. So don't say "sorry" if you bowl a bouncer, just walk back to your mark.' Dennis really took that on.

When he bowled bouncers after that, he wouldn't be sending them over the batsman's head as a warning; no, Dennis would go for the throat and never miss. He'd even do that to the young batters.

Dennis and Trevor were too good to stay in our competition, so I introduced them to Bert Rigg, the president of the Perth Cricket Club. After a year, Bert brought Dennis back and accused me of sending them 'a madman'. He wanted me to help calm him down. With Bert standing there I told Dennis, 'Now listen here, young man, do as these fellas tell you. You're there to learn, and these guys know best and will teach you how to become a better cricketer.' Later that night Dennis and Trevor dropped in to visit me at home, and I said, 'Nah, just keep doing what you're doing. If you get in trouble for being too aggressive, tell them the ball slipped out of your hand.'

We were always really frank with each other. I remember he was playing Shield cricket at the WACA against Victoria, and Dennis was struggling against the four left-handed batsmen they had. He came walking along the boundary, and I said, 'Do you know where the fucking off-stump is?' My mate says, 'You can't talk to Dennis Lillee like that!' He finished up with six or seven wickets for 70-odd, so I guess I could.

Mick Basile, former coach of South Belmont Cricket Club under-16s

As a teenager I barely even left Western Australia, so I was pretty excited to be in Sydney in early 1971 – especially ahead of playing my second Test for Australia.

Dennis as a teenager

I first met Dennis and Trevor in 1965, when I started playing junior cricket for the Perth Cricket Club at Lathlain Park. They were both playing grade cricket, and both would come to Lathlain on Saturday mornings to encourage the younger brigade. Following our junior game, I used to stay on and operate the scoreboard for Perth A Grade, so I got to know the whole Lillee family, including Dennis's grandfather, Len 'Pop' Halifax.

Pop, a former boxing coach, believed that superior fitness enabled sportsmen to reach another level – mentally as well as physically. He pushed Dennis and Trevor to train hard. 'Run, Dennis, run!' was his catch cry, and his grandson did what he was told. I don't know anybody that worked harder to achieve success than Dennis.

Sportsmen of Dennis's era had to have professions and work eight hours a day before going to training. His commitment and work ethic towards training and preparing for a game was ahead of its time. The example he set became the benchmark for the West Australian cricketers who, not coincidentally, I'm sure, became so successful during Dennis's playing career and beyond.

Trevor had far more natural ability than Dennis. He was a very talented opening batsman and leg-spin and medium-pace bowler, but he didn't have the same drive. Dennis was very quick, with no idea of inswingers or outswingers, or leg or off cutters. He just wanted to bowl very fast and frighten batsmen, which he did quite regularly. The brothers were both talked about very early in their careers as potential Western Australia players, but Trevor was drafted into the army and lost interest in cricket, while Dennis continued to train the house down.

Although he bowled very fast it was often with little success, as his accuracy was erratic to say the least. At 16 I was picked to keep wickets for Perth A Grade, and I vividly recall keeping for Dennis in a game against Scarborough where I let through 32 byes off Dennis's bowling.

The Scarborough captain was a famous WA sportsman, Derek Chadwick. 'Chaddy' opened the batting for WA, and he also played over 250 games of Australian Rules football for East Perth. Dennis gained a yard in pace whenever he bowled against state players. On this occasion he was bowling very quickly but all over the shop – both sides of the wicket. The better Chaddy batted, the quicker Dennis bowled; the quicker he bowled the more erratic he got. Chaddy made a polished 70-odd before Dennis finally got him out, but at quite a cost on the scoreboard: eight lots of four byes, which all should have been wides as I had no chance of reaching the ball. I regularly used to question Dennis about his radar and call him a pie chucker!

Wayne Hill, former captain of Perth Cricket Club and West Australian wicketkeeper

No idea where the ball was going

I first met Dennis when he came down to the Perth Cricket Club as a young and green potential fast bowler. I was fortunate enough to be club captain at the time, and my first impressions of Dennis were of someone very quiet and attentive, who was keen to learn but wasn't pushy or big-headed. He had a strong desire to succeed but no clear idea of a pathway. He trained hard, was focused, and was not interested in going out and playing up.

I sensed immediately that he was someone keen to listen, and he took on board every bit of advice given to him. In the early days, he used to come to my home frequently – after matches and nearly always on the evening before the Saturday match. He was constantly asking about cricket, and I usually had to call time on the night and drop him home.

My brother Peter tells the story of one fixture that was abandoned after it rained constantly for nearly 24 hours. It was pretty obvious that there'd be no cricket, and that was confirmed on the radio, but Dennis just wouldn't accept that the match wasn't going ahead. Peter eventually had to drop a very unhappy Dennis home.

He was very naive, young Dennis, and I remember his first pre-season cricket camp, which included a sleepover. On the first morning, Dennis was a bit out of sorts and attracting attention for the wrong reasons. He had a problem, he said, and couldn't get on with the schedule. 'The milk on my Weeties isn't hot. My mum always serves my Weeties with hot milk.' After sorting that issue out, he was ready for the day. He got a bit of ribbing for that, but I noticed how it just slid off him like water off a duck's back, and he never appeared to hold any kind of ill feeling. In hindsight, this characteristic served him well throughout his career, as he was able to harness that response and energy, and use it to effect at a time of his choosing. In fact, I never noticed Dennis getting upset or verbal with anyone – umpires, club officers, teammates or opposition players – during the period we played together.

Our tactics were simple: 'Bowl quick, bowl at the [off-]stumps.' I urged him to convey to the batsman that he was ready to tear in and knock his block off.

During a match, he'd be given the new ball. I went up to his end, stood with him and set an aggressive field. I then went to forward short leg just off the cut strip, and, often just before he started in, I'd say, 'As fast as you can.' This had the double benefit of reminding him of the fundamentals and unnerving the batter.

While Dennis was quick – almost lethal – as a bowler, he was a gentle soul and didn't want to hurt any batter or even cause them distress. Dennis didn't have much of a clue where the ball was going to land when he let it go, and often voiced concern about hitting the batter (I told him that if he knocked them down or hit them, I'd attend to them), or me at forward short leg. I reminded Dennis that if he didn't know where the ball was going,

then the batter definitely had no idea. His percentages certainly improved with experience, and no batter was seriously hurt (though many had bruises and pain to show for their time at the wicket).

I constantly reinforced the need for Dennis to get back quickly to his mark and not loiter around the stumps or seek conversation with fielders – to not run back, but to take purposeful strides then turn around with ball in hand and show the batter he was ready to rip into him. 'Don't give the batter time to compose himself,' I would tell him, 'let him know through body language that you are after him.' He was a quick, efficient and effective learner.

It was a thrill to have such raw talent and such a fiercely determined character in our team. I consider myself lucky to have been in the right place at the right time, and to have had some small part to play in what became the Dennis Lillee legend.

Kevin Taylforth, former captain of Perth Cricket Club

Not sure how I ended up with this image but I kept it because it showed the different points of my delivery and was a useful learning tool before video technology was available to us.

HONK IF YOU'RE PLAYING STATE

JOHN BERTRAND EXPERIENCED A CACOPHONY after he sailed *Australia II* to victory in the 1983 America's Cup at Newport, Rhode Island, when all the surrounding craft honked their horns. I had a similar experience in 1970, although it was in the less salubrious surrounds of Perth's Fletcher Park while I was playing grade cricket, it was equally special.

I was close to state selection for the first time, and the deal was that my father, with his ear glued to the radio, would sound his car horn to let me know if I'd made the team. My hopes had been boosted, with Western Australia's two best fast bowlers, Graham McKenzie and Laurie Mayne, touring India with Australia at the time.

When Dad heard the news that I'd made it, he started beeping his horn madly. Other cars parked around the ground must have been listening in too and immediately joined my father in making an unholy racket. I think it was the best sound I'd ever heard.

And so, aged 20, I was off to play Sheffield Shield cricket in Brisbane. I was determined to bowl as fast as I could, but on the unresponsive Gabba wicket I was spraying my deliveries around a fair bit. I can still remember my first wicket as though it was yesterday – Queensland captain Sam Trimble, caught in close on the leg side by Derek Chadwick.

I picked up another wicket in the second innings and finished with the unflattering figures of 2–60. My captain, Tony Lock, a father figure to me in those early days, was happy enough. He didn't seem to mind that I was a bit wayward at times. All he cared about was that I was trying to bowl really fast.

We played a total of four games on that tour, and with a bag of six wickets in the last game in Adelaide, I returned home with 15 scalps – and a new nickname.

As I spent a lot of time fielding at deep fine leg or third man, Lock often had to adjust exactly where I stood. On one occasion, he must have thought I was a bit slow to react to his command to move, and he shouted, 'Come on, Lil, you're like a flipping old tart!' (or words to that effect). John Inverarity, the ever-alert school teacher, overheard Lock's instruction and in an instant labelled me 'FOT', a nickname that's stuck with me to this day. ●

Pre-season squad camp at Point Peron near Perth. Rod Marsh is wearing a different glove to the one he became so well-known for. I'm second from the right, standing with a mate of mine, the very talented cricketer Les Varis.

BANKING ON CRICKET

MY SELECTION IN AUSTRALIA A, THE Australian seconds squad that Sam Trimble led to New Zealand in 1970, came with some behind-the-scenes drama.

My pop, Len Halifax, telephoned to congratulate me while I was at the bank. Although I'd asked a workmate to take over from me, the branch's accountant took exception to this, told me to get off the phone and, after a few minutes, just leaned over and cut the line.

I was ropeable, as you can imagine. I called my pop back and continued the conversation for another couple of minutes, while the accountant had steam coming out of his ears. His face went purple, and I began to see my career in banking leaching down the drain.

I was marched into the manager's office and lectured about cricket dominating my thoughts. I told them it wasn't but could in the future,

because I was hell-bent on pursuing my passion. It was a brave or stupid thing to say, because I was going well there and there wasn't a living to be made out of cricket. In time I would leave the bank, but the search for work that would allow me to continue playing cricket as well as support my family would remain one of the big struggles of my early career.

In New Zealand I played in only the last of the three unofficial Tests and took just one wicket on a featherbed Wellington pitch – that of Glenn Turner. One unfortunate incident from that tour has stuck in my mind. After I misfielded my captain, Sam Trimble, raced over to me and, while the crowd watched, gave me a lesson on how to pick up the ball correctly. That was something Ian Chappell would never have done. A quiet word afterwards or maybe tuition at the nets would have been a better way to handle it. ●

Some bank colleagues were happy for me when I got selected to tour New Zealand for Australia A. Others, not so much.

Winding up the new guy

I enjoyed the fact that our Test careers followed the same trajectory, and pretty much began and ended at the same time. Dennis and I spent a lot of time together, had a lot of fun together, enjoyed a lot of success together and endured failures together, which only made us more determined not to be on the losing end. Dennis was a big part of the success we had in that era. If you needed a wicket, Dennis was always the man you'd go to. He won many matches on his own just through effort, sheer bloody-mindedness and such a strong will. Always steaming in, never giving anything but 100 per cent.

> But I wasn't so sure of him at the start. The first time I saw him over a protracted period was on a 1970 tour of New Zealand. He was quick, but ungainly and all over the place. And he was unbelievably gullible.

We got into the habit of buying a bottle of wine at lunch over that tour, following the lead of Graeme Watson, who was older and much more worldly than the rest of us. When it was my turn to buy, I sniffed the wine like I'd seen people do. Dennis, sitting beside me, chimed in with, 'You'd be a bit of a toff, wouldn't you? What's all that shit about?'

I pretended to take offence, and said, 'Listen, Dennis, you can't go around saying that to people. I happen to be a wine

taster.' He pulled his head in a little bit. The next day, I was at the same table as him for lunch again, and he says, 'I thought you said you worked with Coca Cola bottlers.'

'Well, I do now,' I said, 'but I used to work as a wine taster.'

'So, what do you do at Coca Cola?' he said.

'*Now* I'm a Coke taster.'

'Bullshit!' he barked.

'There you go again, Dennis. You can't just go around calling "bullshit" on everything people say. We're just having a conversation here.' And he pulled his head in again.

'What do you do?' I asked, bringing the conversation back to a civil tone. He told me he was a bank teller.

'What a coincidence,' I said. 'I used to be a bank teller. Until I got caught with my hand in the till.'

'Jesus!' he exclaimed, 'That must have been bad.'

'Ah, it was okay,' I said. 'My father was the bank manager. He just swept the whole thing under the carpet and I left quietly.' Dennis just nodded seriously. I realised then that I had Dennis hook, line and sinker, and that he'd believe pretty much anything I said. So I told a few of the older players and we cooked up a plan. After the tour Graeme Watson was heading off to get married, and he had a huge wad of US dollar travellers' cheques on him. We decided these cheques would go missing, and the fallen bank teller would become the suspect.

Terry Jenner spread the rumour that I couldn't be trusted: 'You know about his history, the bloke is a kleptomaniac.' Now, I don't want to cast aspersions on fast bowlers, but it was mainly Alan 'Froggy' Thomson and Dennis Lillee that fell for this – and in a big way. Dennis was even trying to stick up for me, apparently.

The next part of the plan was that Terry would convince Froggy to search my gear. Off they went while the rest of us were at dinner, and I could see them sneak away. I was rooming with Terry, so he directed Froggy to my bag and, sure enough, he found the travellers' cheques. He marched back to the dining table, where there were about 15 of us sitting at one long table in the public dining room, and he threw the traveller's cheques on the table, booming, 'I found them!'

The team manager, Frank Bryant, who was in on the lark, told him to keep the noise down. Next thing, we're having a team meeting where I'm to be confronted with the evidence and asked to hand back my blazer and cap and get a ticket home. I'm last into the room, looking sheepish, while several of the players couldn't come in at all because they were laughing so hard, but I could see them looking in the window. The boys in the room were biting their fists, trying to keep serious, while Dennis shook his head in disbelief. Froggy had to be physically restrained from leaping across the room and knocking my block off (as a fellow Victorian, he was sticking up for Graeme).

Frank started, and addressed the 'rather serious issue we have to deal with', talking about how even though my grandfather captained Australia and my brother was playing for Australia, this was not something that could be taken lightly. Then he mentions the travellers' cheques and Froggy yells out, 'Yeah, and I found them in that so-and-so's bloody suitcase.' Meanwhile, Dennis just kept shaking his head.

I said, 'Look, I'm sorry, I've got a bit of history. I saw the traveller's cheques and I couldn't … couldn't …' Well, actually, I couldn't hold it together anymore, and when I started to crack the whole room fell into an uproar. I remember as clear as day the penny dropping with Dennis, and he just leapt up, yelled, 'You absolute bastards, you've done me!' and stormed out of the room.

Greg Chappell, former captain of Australia, 87 Tests

Not a bad second XI! From memory, at least nine players had played or would play Test cricket.

POPPING THE QUESTION

IT HAD BEEN A VERY FORTUNATE DECISION OF MY mother's one afternoon to send me to the deli to buy bread. There I noticed a very attractive young woman who was also on an errand, and I made it my business to find out a bit more about her. Her name was Helen, and she lived in the house behind ours. (I wasn't slow off the mark; we had just moved into the area!)

We liked each other straight away, and she immediately had a steadying influence on me. As things developed, we knew we wanted to get married. It was during the Australia A tour of New Zealand that I began looking at engagement rings.

The most nerve-racking thing was observing the formalities of the time and asking Helen's father, Bob. At lunch at Helen's house one day, I decided to act. When Bob left the lunch table, I sprang up and followed him out the door.

'Bob, Bob, can I have a word please?' I called after him.

'No worries,' he said, 'just let me pop into the loo.'

I spent 20 very awkward minutes shuffling around in the corridor, unsure of whether to stay or abandon my post. When he eventually came out, I blurted, 'I want to know if Helen and I can get married?'

'Sure,' he said, 'no problem,' and walked straight back into the dining room. I'd been building up to that for weeks! I have a feeling he knew exactly what he was doing.

Although Helen was only 17 and I was 20, both our sets of parents seemed to think we were mature enough, and both were very fond of their prospective in-laws. And Helen and I were certainly very much in love. ●

TOP: Shopping for a ring on the Australia A tour of New Zealand in 1970, with teammates Geoff 'Hatch' Davies and Alan 'Froggy' Thomson.

BOTTOM LEFT: We often went on picnics in my FE Holden, but the ground here was very muddy, hence the piggyback – not quite Sir Walter Raleigh!

BOTTOM RIGHT: The best day of my life, and the love of my life, Helen.

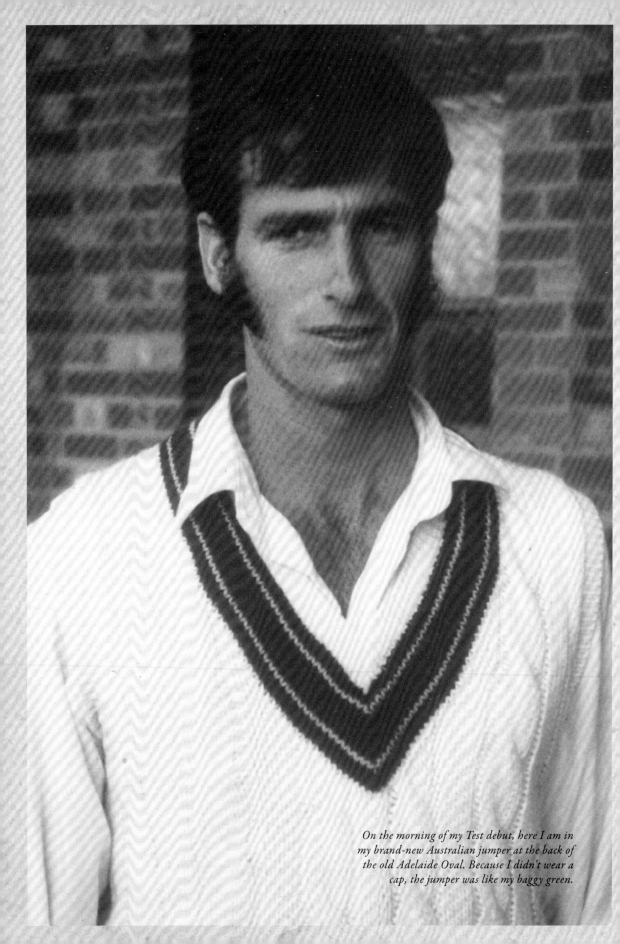

On the morning of my Test debut, here I am in my brand-new Australian jumper at the back of the old Adelaide Oval. Because I didn't wear a cap, the jumper was like my baggy green.

— 3 —

BAGGY GREEN

There's always some luck involved with success, and there certainly was with my Test selection. When I got close to a call-up I started trying too hard, lost my rhythm and nearly blew the chance completely.

Knocking Geoff Boycott's cap off, pre-helmets, announced to the world that I could attain great pace. It was WA v England in an early tour warm-up game, well in advance of the upcoming Test series. I wasn't picked until the last Test match, though.

A SURPRISE CALL-UP

STORM CLOUDS WERE BREWING WHEN RAY Illingworth led his England players Down Under in 1970–71, with fiery Sussex fast bowler John Snow heading his armoury. Encouraged by my blooding in New Zealand, I'd hoped to be in the mix during an Ashes season that saw a seventh Test added after the scheduled third Test in Melbourne was washed out without a ball being bowled.

But things didn't go to plan right from the start, and I managed just six wickets for plenty in a miserable four-match Sheffield Shield tour of the eastern states. Things went from bad to worse, and in Western Australia's first game on our return Barry Richards helped himself to 356 runs for South Australia, and I finished with 0–117.

The following week I was relegated to 12th man for the state game against Illingworth's Marylebone Cricket Club line-up. I thought my brief Sheffield Shield career might be over, but luckily for me Graham McKenzie pulled out at the last minute. I was back in the side.

Even when you bowl thousands and thousands of balls during a long career, there are a few you simply never forget, and this match featured one of them. With my very first delivery, I knocked dour opener Geoff Boycott's cap flying.

In that match I seemed to relax a little more and was able to bowl quite fast during the second innings. I finished it a much happier man after getting Boycott out for nine and Colin Cowdrey for six. In Western Australia's next match I teamed up with Bob Massie for the first time, and we finished with 14 wickets between us. I was feeling good.

But for the first four Tests of that Ashes series, selectors used Graham McKenzie, Alan 'Froggy' Thomson, Alan Connolly and Ross Duncan for new ball duties. Meanwhile Snow was on a rampage, taking 26 wickets including 6–114 in the first innings in Brisbane and 7–40 in the second innings at the SCG. England had gone 1–0 up and looked on track to regain the little urn.

Selectors certainly did things differently in those days, because I only heard about my Test debut call-up during a WA v Country XI over the WACA's loudspeaker system. I was sitting in the dressing room when the team for the sixth Test in Adelaide was announced. I was in the team and fifth cab off the rank for the summer. Teammates and other supporters poured in to shake my hand, along with my parents and grandfather, who were at the ground; Helen arrived during the tea interval. And so I was off to Adelaide along with Rod Marsh, the only other West Australian in the Test team.

When I arrived I immediately became aware of the media hype that was suggesting I was the answer to Snow in a bouncer war. I was aghast – I knew I couldn't win such a war against a bowler as great as John Snow!

Sir Donald Bradman, then still a selector, knew exactly what was going on in my head and he took me aside for a most welcome chat before the Test began.

'You've been picked to bowl as you normally would – forget this bumper war business,' he told me. 'Just keep the ball up to the batsman and bowl normally, and I'm sure you'll do well.' It was among the best pieces of advice I was ever given in cricket.

Froggy Thomson took the first over with the wind, which at least gave me a bit more time to compose myself, but I still struggled in my early overs and had to wait a long time for success. In fact, England was 2–276 when I finally got John Edrich, on 130, to edge a delivery to Keith Stackpole in the slips. At the end of the day I was pretty satisfied with my figures – 1–41 off 14 overs.

The next day, with the wind at my back, I was bowling with more rhythm. I picked up nightwatchman Alan Knott early. I then added Illingworth, Snow and Bob Willis to finish with 5–84 from 28.3 overs in my first Test innings. I was overjoyed.

The seventh Test in Sydney, though, was one I would like to forget. I guess I tried to bowl too fast and so I lost my all-important rhythm, finishing with only three wickets.

That, of course, became the infamous Illingworth walk-off Test (Ian Chappell's first as skipper) after Snow flattened Terry Jenner with a bouncer and was grabbed by a spectator while fielding near the fence. I had walked to the crease to replace the injured Jenner, his blood still on the pitch. To say I was nervous is a massive understatement!

We ended up losing that Test, and the Ashes, but the disappointment of it all instilled some urgency in me – I desperately wanted revenge against the old enemy. ●

LINE AND LENGTH
IN LANCASHIRE

HAVING NEARLY KNOCKED GEOFF BOYCOTT'S head off in Perth early in the season, I was keen to pick his brains in Sydney at the end of the volatile 1970–71 summer. Geoff suggested that I play county cricket in England during the off-season. I was open to his idea, but decided the daily grind of doing that would be too much at that time, and instead I opted to have a season with Haslingden in the Lancashire League.

The furthest I'd gone from home before was New Zealand, so it was a great experience for Helen and me (although it was pretty difficult at the time). I encountered many characters, including a blind man who used to stand by the sightscreen with his pint, shouting abuse and telling me what I was doing wrong.

One day I pitched a quick one right in front, hit the pads and screamed my appeal to the umpire. The umpire gave him out, but the batsman just stood there, not moving. I asked him what the hell he was doing, and he just said, 'I think you've broken my leg.' He had to be carried off.

I gained valuable experience bowling in strange conditions in the 20 or so games I played there. The most important lesson I learnt was the need to bowl a good line and length on slow pitches. I took only 68 wickets and finished 11th on the list, but it stood me in good stead. ●

The tip where I worked while playing cricket in Lancashire. And when I say tip, I don't mean it wasn't a nice place – it was an actual rubbish tip. Oh the glamour of being an international cricketer in the 1970s.

Slippery fingers at Haslingden

I saw Dennis make his debut for Australia against Ray Illingworth's England Team on television – although raw he was certainly quick and aggressive, and so it created quite a stir when Dennis signed for Haslingden to play in the Lancashire League for the 1971 season.

Helen and Dennis created an even bigger stir the day after they arrived, with the story going around the town that they needed their bed repaired after it had collapsed on their first night. 'No jet lag there then,' said one of the lads. They both became very popular, although it was soon obvious that Dennis was not over just for

a holiday but to gain as much experience as he could to further his career. He made it plain that he expected us to train to get fitter, which was a shock to some of the lads who'd previously trained on 10 pints a night. Off the field Dennis was great company, very quiet, and he drank very little – the opposite to his aggressive approach on the field.

We played a game at home versus Ramsbottom, who had Bapu Nadkarni, an Indian Test player, as professional. Dennis had a couple of early wickets and his tail was up. When Nadkarni came in to bat, he deliberately took ages to make his way to

The Haslingden Cricket Team of 1971, where I played in the Lancashire League and to whom training was an alien concept. (I'm bottom row, second from the left, and the guy sitting next to me on the far left is Malcolm Grindrod.) The company was definitely of a higher standard than the cricket. They were middling when I arrived, and middling by the time I left. However, Helen and I made some long-lasting friendships and we had a wonderful time. I also learnt a great deal about bowling in very different and difficult conditions.

the middle, and then, to take the heat off the situation, he took his time and said, 'Good afternoon,' to each of the close fielders crowding around the bat.

Dennis by this time had steam coming out of his ears, wanting to keep up the momentum. He finally ran in to bowl and sent it fizzing past Nadkarni's nose, following through with, 'Good fucking evening, Bapu! What kept you?' Nadkarni just looked at Dennis and said, 'Now, then, I am being nice to everybody. Why are you not being nice to me?' Dennis was left speechless, probably for the only time that season.

Away at Colne later that summer, they had two brothers playing for them and, from a distance, they looked identical. One of them opened the batting and proceeded to play and miss almost every delivery. If he did hit the ball, it was off the edge, and Dennis was soon exasperated. Dennis eventually clean-bowled him and sent him on his way with a few choice words. The incoming batsman was his brother. Dennis started his long run-up, only to stop halfway and yell, 'What the bloody hell is going on? I've just bowled you – now fuck off.' We had to tell Dennis that he was the opening batter's brother, but he took some convincing.

We did not have a good season, and Dennis's figures were only moderate, but it has to be said that he would have had more wickets if our slip fielders had not had such slippery fingers.

Malcolm Grindrod, former Haslingden teammate

On the day of my Test debut, looking a little less intense when posing with a bat.

DIZZY HEIGHTS
AND GARY SOBERS

WITH THE 1971–72 TOUR BY SOUTH AFRICA called off because of apartheid, the Australian Cricket Board announced that a 'Rest of the World' team, captained by the mighty Gary Sobers, would visit instead.

With the 1972 tour of England looming it was crucial to have quality opposition that summer under new captain Ian Chappell. The first game of the Rest of the World series in Brisbane was rain-affected, and I finished with the meagre return of three wickets for 111.

I was relishing the prospect of facing them again at the WACA. Australia got off to a flying start, scoring 349 runs on the first day. The next morning, however, when I should have been raring to bowl, I woke up feeling dreadful. I didn't feel like getting out of bed, never mind leading the Australian attack.

But the gods were on my side, because the wicket had sweated overnight and promised to be extra fast. The first delivery I sent down snapped me out of my lethargy. Short of a length, it flew so fast and high that Rod Marsh had to stretch every sinew in his body to drag it down.

The fourth ball also climbed, and Sunil 'Sunny' Gavaskar gloved it to Marsh. After four overs, two for 29, I started feeling crook again and asked Ian Chappell for a spell. Totally unsympathetic, he just replied, 'See if you can bowl a couple more.'

I gritted my teeth and continued. Nothing happened in my next over, but suddenly the flood gates opened and I got another six wickets for no runs in the space of 15 balls. We had the star-studded outfit back in the dressing room before lunch for only 59. I got a career-best eight for 29 and had the uncharitable Ian Chappell to thank!

That WACA wicket was probably the fastest I ever bowled on, but my teammates deserve a lot of the credit because they took some truly remarkable catches.

I sat down in the dressing room, totally exhausted but feeling pretty good about

ABOVE: Sunil Gavaskar avoids a bouncer in the match between Australia and the Rest of the World team. We both got centuries in that match, but his was more memorable than mine – I took 3–111! But I had bowled quick, and it was enough to get selected for the next match.

OPPOSITE: The WACA scoreboard shows my career-best figures, thanks to the fastest wicket I've ever bowled on, against the star-studded Rest of the World team. Funnily, I wasn't feeling well and asked Ian Chappell to take me off after I'd taken two wickets. Luckily he told me to keep playing. I took the last six wickets, including Gary Sobers, in 15 balls, bowling every delivery flat-out.

At the WACA, 1971, after taking 8–29 against the Rest of the World team. Australia made 341 and our opponents made only 59. We made them follow on. Farokh Engineer, one of the openers, got the dubious record of being the first player to be dismissed twice in one session (two hours). He didn't live it down for many years.

having got through it. And then Ian Chappell announced that he was enforcing the follow-on! Out I went again and picked up one more wicket, making it nine for the session. The unfortunate Farokh Engineer was thus out twice before lunch in a first-class match, something which would not have made him sleep well that night.

I finished the WACA match with 12 wickets before we headed to Melbourne, where the axiom 'the glorious uncertainty of cricket' was painfully proven. The man to inflict the misery was the stung captain, Sobers, who had unbeaten scores of 20 and 15 in Brisbane. I got him for a first innings duck in Perth, and he managed 33 in his second dig.

I was thinking, *How easy is this?* when I got Sobers for another nought first time around at the MCG, and I was so close to getting him again, hooking in my first over of the second innings. But that was when the mighty man stepped up, as if to say, 'Enough of this nonsense.' Sobers, with no member of the Australian attack spared, peeled off 254 majestic runs in 376 minutes, with two sixes and 35 fours.

Don Bradman proclaimed, 'I believe Gary Sobers's innings was probably the best ever seen in Australia. The people who saw Sobers have enjoyed one of the historic events of cricket. They were privileged to have such an experience.' Certainly, in my very limited time in the game, I had to agree. Still to this day it stands among the best I've seen. ●

Watershed moment

I've often described Dennis Lillee as a captain's dream and a batsman's nightmare. On the occasions when I was accused of over-bowling Australia's premier fast bowler, I responded by asking, 'Have you ever tried to take a bone off a Doberman?'

Lillee was everything a captain would want in a fast bowler: he was tireless, highly motivated and extremely skilful, and his iron will ensured he was always the last player on the field to believe victory was impossible.

At The Oval in 1972 – a watershed Test for a team that went on to dominate world cricket – we gathered to congratulate Ashley Mallett on taking England's ninth second-innings wicket, with our opponents holding a lead of 241. It was the penultimate day of a gruelling six-day Test, and Lillee had already delivered 56 overs in the

match and 250 for the series. 'We can't let these bastards score another run,' barked Lillee. 'It's already a difficult chase,' he added before storming back to his mark.

Lillee then charged in and bowled Alan Knott, who was well set on 63. That final wicket was gained with pure willpower; the delivery didn't deviate, it was far from Dennis's fastest that day, and yet it crashed through Knott's usually solid defence and rearranged the furniture.

The delivery that captured Knott's wicket epitomised Lillee the fast bowler. He was not only a talented wicket-taker but he could also inspire a team with his self-belief. Australia went on to win a thrilling Test at The Oval and level the series at two-all.

Ian Chappell, former captain of Australia, 75 Tests

Bob Massie, Doug Walters, Ian Chappell, David Colley, Greg Chappell and myself during the second Test at Lord's, 1972. There was incredible spirit in that team.

Ever the enthusiast

Dennis had intent and ambition in abundance, but he was also gullible when he started. On his first interstate trip, when we were representing Western Australia, I recall sharing a two-berth compartment with him on an overnight train from Sydney to Brisbane. The second bed folded down from the wall and a narrow luggage rack was high on the other side. As the time approached for us to get some sleep, DK wondered aloud where he, as the newer member of the duo, was to sleep. I pointed to the luggage rack and told him I'd loan him a pillow. As he began his climb into the luggage rack, I pressed the button and the second bed slowly descended to a horizontal position. He was both relieved and good-naturedly amused. It wasn't long before he 'read the play' and was right to the fore in the leg-pulling stakes.

How good was Dennis Lillee, and why? Well, he was the stand-out fast bowler of his generation; an aggressive, fiery bowler who was genuinely fast, and a fierce competitor with a never-say-die attitude. What made him stand apart? His sheer pace, the way in which he adapted when his pace declined, his intelligence and his will – perhaps more than anything else, it was his will. Many players prepared well, tried hard and were very determined, but Dennis took all of these things to a higher level. A significantly higher level. Nobody else trained anything like Dennis did. With 'Run, Dennis, run!' ringing in his ears from his grandfather, Pop Halifax, Dennis ran, and ran, and ran. He became superfit. He was able to come back again and again on the hottest and most demanding of days and bowl flat-out. He was a captain's dream, and he won huge respect from his team (and opponents) not only for his bowling prowess, but for his efforts and attitude as well.

At times, DKL batted well and to good effect. This was not the case in the fourth Test at Leeds in 1972. He joined me, on 26 not out, with Australia 9–146. Ever the enthusiast, Dennis strode to the wicket but came to me at the non-striker's end for a chat and a 'rev-up'. 'You're going really well, mate. I'll hold up an end and you can do the scoring. I'll stick with you.'

He then went to the striker's end to face Geoff Arnold, took guard with great care, looked around the field and then settled over his bat. To the first ball he played a perfect forward defence, bat and pad close together and head down over the ball. Proud of his start, he looked up at me, nodded and gave a little fist pump. To the next ball – the last of the over, pitched on a length on off-stump – he took a 'head-up' wild swing that resulted in an easy catch at cover. 'Sorry, mate, just lost concentration for a bit. But it was there to hit,' he said, running off to get his bowling boots on. Over the years we've enjoyed reminding each other of this 'inglorious innings' of his.

John Inverarity, six Tests for Australia, former captain of Western Australia, and former chairman of selectors for Cricket Australia

There was plenty of downtime on tour. The team decided we'd see who could grow the best mo, which had never even occurred to me before. What I lacked in style, I certainly made up for in a lifetime commitment to the moustache.

L–R: Ross Edwards; Paul Sheahan; me; Greg Chappell. England, 1972.

Caught Marsh, bowled Lillee. It occurred 95 times – still a record. This time it's Alan Knott, a great English wicketkeeper and a very handy batsman.

TRYING TOO HARD

TOWARDS THE END OF THE REST OF THE WORLD series in 1972, when it seemed I was at the top of my game, a good-natured taunt from Ian Chappell triggered a protracted chain of events that almost forced me into permanent retirement.

With the series at one-all, I was plugging away in the tourists' second innings on an unresponsive SCG pitch. Ian, unimpressed with the pace I was generating, walked up to me and said, 'Look, if I want someone to bowl spinners, I'll ask Terry Jenner.'

I stormed back to the top of my mark, determined to bowl the fastest delivery I had ever sent down, just to prove my captain wrong. I hurtled in and let fly a delivery to

The ball hit Boycott on the shoulder, then popped up and over his shoulder and amazingly fell onto the stumps. You can see Ian Chappell's reaction at first slip. Like me, he couldn't believe our luck.

Sunny Gavaskar that had him playing an extremely hurried shot.

But my excitement was replaced with a spear of pain that shot through the base of my spine. I somehow managed to finish the over and then hobbled from the ground.

A muscle problem was the initial diagnosis. I flew out to Perth almost immediately, where a doctor gave me a set of stretching exercises designed to ease muscle pain. He made me rest for a fortnight, but I had to get back in the nets after that because it was getting close to picking the team for the tour to England.

I felt I had to play a Sheffield Shield match to ensure my spot, and although my figures weren't too flash, the effort was enough to get me on the plane.

Not surprisingly it was freezing when we arrived. The first county game was against Worcestershire, and I took great care in warming up before I sent down a single ball in the nets. Despite my efforts, the sharp pain I was getting at the base of my spine was way too frequent when I stretched out.

Word came from a specialist in London that I was suffering from inflammation, and that I wasn't to worry if I experienced a bit of pain when I tried to bowl fast. But nothing seemed to work, and at one stage I broke down and cried with disappointment and frustration. In fact, if it hadn't been for the support and understanding I received from Keith Stackpole and, later, my skipper, I probably would have packed up and gone home.

I played in the following games against Lancashire and Nottinghamshire with bursts of encouraging signs, but the pain returned. It was decided that I would return to London and have a specialist manipulate my body under a general anaesthetic.

After a lot of rest, I started bowling again. At first things didn't seem to be working, but during the second innings against Hampshire I was delighted that I was able to generate considerable pace.

Against the MCC at Lord's I got Geoff Boycott LBW through sheer pace, and I was right for the first Test at Old Trafford where we got beaten on a 'greentop' (my figures were 2–40 and 6–66).

Then came 'Massie's match' at Lord's. Although I thought I bowled as well as I ever had, Bob was just sensational and finished with 8–84 and 8–53. We were two mighty proud West Australians, and my four wickets made sure that us 'sandgropers' finished with the lot to level the series one-all.

The Trent Bridge Test was drawn, and England won by nine wickets at Headingley. It is generally thought that Chappell's young team came of age by winning the final Test at The Oval by five wickets to square the series. Ian and his brother Greg scored 118 and 113 respectively in Australia's first innings and, on an old-fashioned Oval wicket (i.e. fast bowlers' graveyard), I managed 5–58 and 5–123 for a series total of 31 wickets. That was a record for an Aussie bowler in an Ashes series at that point, and I rate it as one of my best performances ever in Test cricket.

I was on top of the world after that, but everything was about to come crashing down. ●

Our 1972 win was celebrated in the usual fashion.

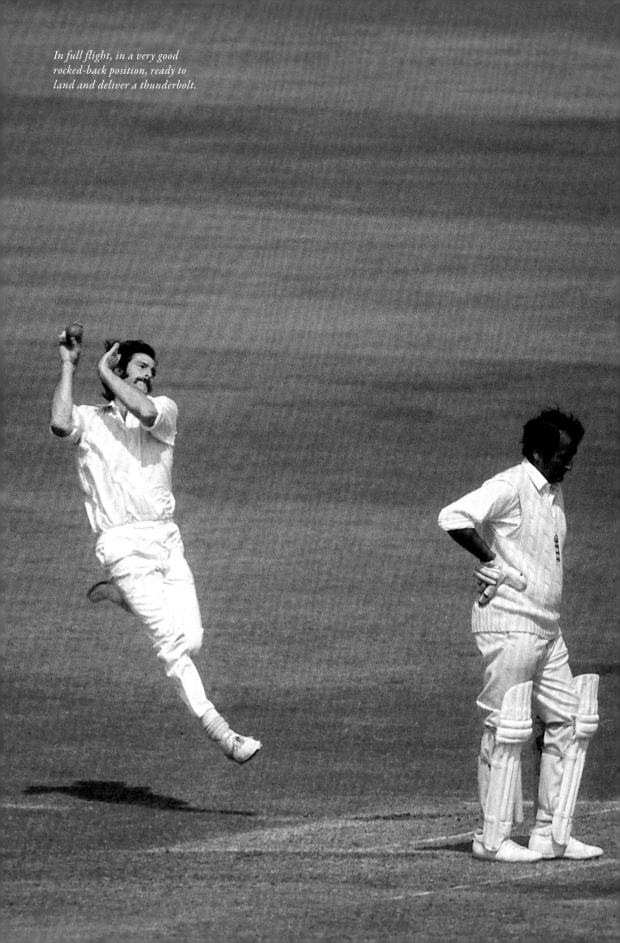

In full flight, in a very good rocked-back position, ready to land and deliver a thunderbolt.

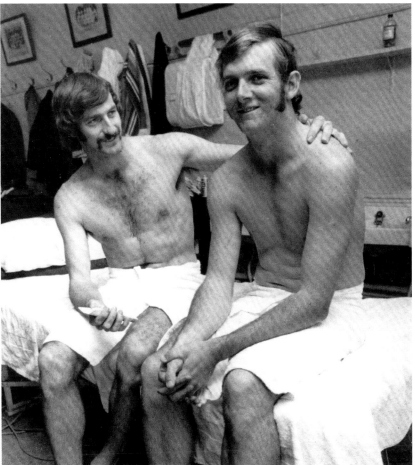

TOP: I got five wickets and looks like Rod got six catches. We are being congratulated by our 1972 tour manager, Ray Steele.

BOTTOM: Congratulating Bob Massie for his 16-wicket haul in the Lord's Test in 1972. We got the whole 20 wickets between us.

CAPTAIN'S RUN

WHEN MY DREAM HAD COME TRUE AND I WAS actually playing for Australia I was pretty fanatical about keeping myself in top shape, even if my teammates didn't seem so fussed.

I would walk off the MCG after having bowled a significant number of overs, knowing full well that I would be tossed the cherry again first thing the next morning. We only had home team 'rubbers' in the rooms in those days; they were shared by both teams and, with respect, not up to physiotherapist standard. So while my teammates were winding down, I'd book an appointment with a physio plus a taxi to get me there (and then another taxi back to the hotel where the team was staying).

It seems ludicrous by today's standards, but I had to organise and pay for all of this myself, and I didn't get one cent of reimbursement from the Australian Cricket Board. I just knew it had to be done.

If a day's play was washed out, that night I would run up and down the corridor of the team hotel to maintain fitness and muscle tone. And if rain meant no practise wickets were available, I would 'shadow bowl' wherever I could find a corridor.

At the end of the 1972 Tour of the UK, Ian Chappell and I had a few days of R&R in London and he invited me to join him for a run. I was shocked – I had never seen him even do a lap of an oval! I relished the chance to impress my captain and planned on leaving him for dead on the road.

After half a kilometre at a good clip, I was surprised to see that he was still at my heels. So I increased the pace for the remaining 7 kilometres and didn't even look back again, sure he'd fade and have to stop. For good measure, I put in a gut-busting last 200 or 300 metres at the finish and was utterly amazed when Ian finished only a few paces behind me.

He just said he also trained extremely hard but at odd hours, when the team wasn't around. To this day I wonder if Ian could have gone past me on that run and was just doing the right thing as leader. As he showed, you've really got to drive that level of fitness and hard work yourself – you can't do it for anyone else. ●

This is one image people had of Ian Chappell, but you don't become the captain of Australia and have a career like his without being supremely fit and fiercely focused. Here he is at a photo call with England captain Ray Illingworth on that 1972 Tour.

Many people said I was the reincarnation of Fred Spofforth, and we certainly look a little alike in this primitive attempt at 'photoshopping' produced by one of my teammates.

Back home with family after being away for nearly six months during the 1972 Ashes tour.

TOP: Pictured with Dad and Pop (who'd been barracking for the Poms). Although it looks very small in proportion to my dad's hands, that's actually a jug he's holding, while Pop and I have middies. This was a set-up for the photo because at that time I rarely drank alcohol.

RIGHT and OPPOSITE: It was always good to get home after a tour to see my family again, especially the two most important women in my life: Helen and Mum.

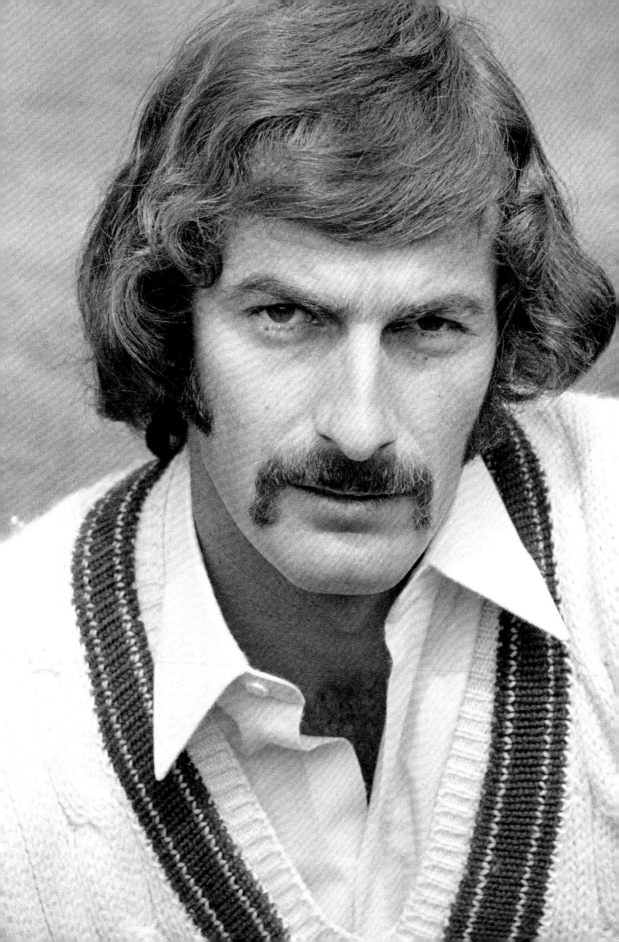

Immersed in conversation

The first time I saw Dennis Lillee in old Blighty, he was clutching a soft drink and making small talk with dignitaries and stargazers at Australia House on The Strand in London.

My second sighting of the nascent champion was in his pokey bathroom around the corner at the Waldorf Hotel. Such was the interest in the long-haired, moustachioed teetotaller with the gift of speed that an interview could be granted from the bath when time was of the essence.

This was April 1972 when, in the main, sporting life was uncomplicated if not innocent, and trust between elite players and the media was absolute. In truth, these were simpler and more satisfying days – at least for the scribes and snappers, for this was also the time the game's finest players were paid a pittance plus a laundry allowance, and their rights and entitlements were routinely disregarded – even abused – by a crusty and unworldly establishment. In time, the whiff of revolution became cool gales carried on the wild winds of change. In 1977, the World Series Cricket (WSC) revolution irrevocably changed the game.

History shows that Dennis was not only a peerless fast bowler but a prime mover of media mogul Kerry Packer's WSC movement. Courageous, intensely competitive and occasionally bloody-minded, Dennis was driven: driven to be the best, driven to defy serious injury, driven to defy all the odds and driven to defy the game's administrators, who he often considered to be as heartless as they were inept. And much like his beloved captain, Ian Chappell, he is for the most part unforgiving. Such was the

sense of injustice and depth of hurt he felt in his pomp. For all his success and fame, he never forgot what it was like to be sneered at by the game's bosses. Even later in life, in the comfort of his suite as president of the Western Australian Cricket Association, he remembered what life was like on the shop floor. His memory is as long as it is good.

A testament to Lillee's greatness as a cricketer is his striking relevance to the cricket community and broader society more than 30 years after his retirement from the Test match arena. While he jealously guards his privacy, he has long turned the heads of advertisers and marketers as well as passers-by wherever he goes.

While he acknowledges the indisputable success of World Series Cricket and proudly accepts a share of responsibility for propelling the game from the 19th to the 21st century, he readily admits to moments of nostalgia.

As a keen observer and an international coach of renown, he has seen the game evolve at dizzying speed. At times, this has left him breathless, and mindful of less congested and frenetic summers when the sporting community was patient and respectful, and mainstream media was discreet and thoughtful, and social media was beyond even the wildest imagination.

These were balmy days when players and scribes had a healthy respect for each other's roles and obligations, and an interview could be happily, harmlessly given from the bath.

Mike Coward, senior Australian cricket writer

A thunderbolt at the MCG.

-- 4 --

BREAKING DOWN

I made the most of my start for Australia but it was at a pace I just could not sustain. In fact, it was very nearly the end of my career.

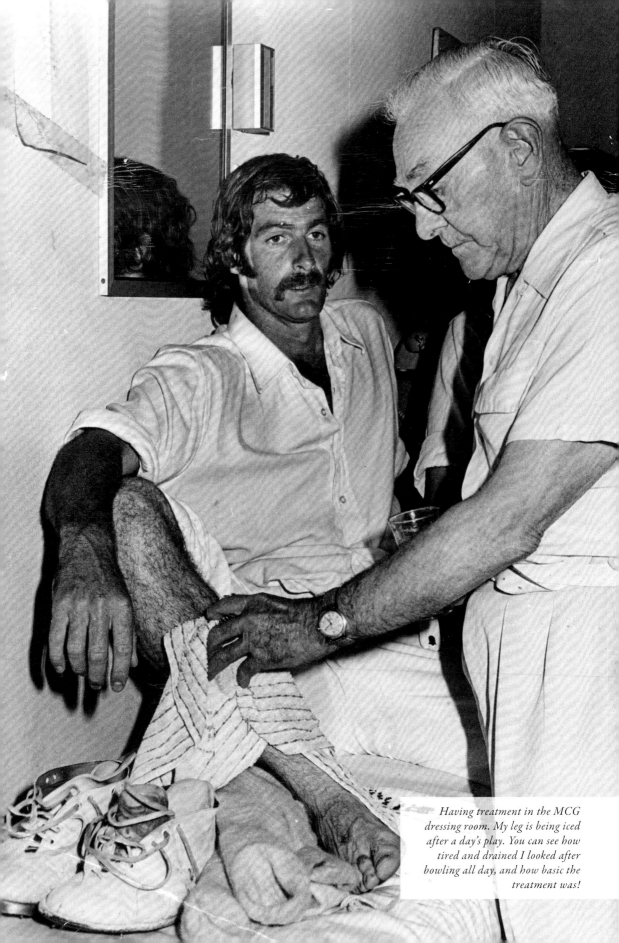

Having treatment in the MCG dressing room. My leg is being iced after a day's play. You can see how tired and drained I looked after bowling all day, and how basic the treatment was!

HARD TIMES

I T WAS AN AMAZING FEELING TO WALK OFF THE Oval in August 1972 having defeated Ray Illingworth's England by five wickets. But I'd have to call on that feeling of elation for comfort many times over the next two years, which were an absolute misery for me.

What cricket I managed to play was racked with pain and uncertainty, until the game was shut down for me completely. I thought it was curtains for my international career.

There'd been little time for rest after the 1972 Ashes tour. I got through the first two Tests against Pakistan in Adelaide and Melbourne with a modest return of eight wickets from 63 overs. I was weary by the time I reached Sydney and, after feeling more back pain while bowling in the nets, it was no surprise that during the first innings my back gave way again.

A doctor advised me to rest up for the remainder of the match, but I felt duty-bound to help out when Pakistan batted a second time. I plugged away at far from top pace for figures of 3–68 while Max Walker did the damage in the 52 run win with 6–15. At one stage in that match Ian Chappell said he would give me a rest, but I told him I had to keep going because there was no coming back once I cooled down. However, it was a mistake to bowl in the second innings, and I was very sore afterwards.

I'm not sure if I was fit enough to go to the West Indies in 1973, but things went reasonably well early in the tour. I played in the drawn first Test in Jamaica but failed to take a wicket

while conceding 132 runs from 32 overs. We moved to Antigua to play the Leeward Islands. It was there that I broke down completely, and didn't bowl another ball in a game on tour. (In Montserrat, after he said I had bugged him about it long enough, Ian Chappell put me in as opening batsman. The West Indies bowlers thought it was Christmas and, realising I wouldn't be able to retaliate, they peppered me bouncers and yorkers in the most torrid time I've ever had at the crease.)

Each island on the tour had its own 'back expert', and so began a merry-go-round of misery. Each physician had a new or different solution, and advised me to have injections, or manipulations under anaesthetic, or to just bowl through it. The latter was impossible.

Fortunately after weeks of playing hit-and-miss I met radiologist Dr Rudi Webster, who was himself a former fast bowler. Rudi X-rayed my spine and discovered the telltale signs of three tiny fractures on two of my vertebrae. He was the only person who suspected fractures (they were not known to be a common sport injury) because they had finished his own cricket career.

Back in Perth, Dr Bill Gilmour, a leading orthopaedic surgeon, X-rayed me again to find the specific area. He encased me in plaster from my buttocks to the base of my chest for six weeks. It would have been impossible to cope without Helen's help. The next step was an aluminium ribbed harness, and while it was just as uncomfortable and restrictive as the plaster, I was at least able to take it off and have a shower.

Many months of complete rest were needed before we would know whether I could ever bowl again – never mind bowl at the top level. It would require incredible discipline and dedication and, to be honest, there were times I didn't think I had it in me.

When I felt mobile again, I opted to play the 1973–74 summer as captain-coach of the Perth Cricket Club. I intended not to bowl a single ball during that entire period. I concentrated on my batting and finished the season with more than 600 runs, which wasn't far behind the best of them in that season in first grade.

Dr Gilmour conducted regular check-ups and assured us the healing process was coming along well. My old high school teacher Frank Pyke, who'd moved on to the University of Western Australia's physical education department, designed a rehabilitation program for me. I followed this program meticulously for around a year, and it became the basis of my core strength exercises for the rest of my career. Frank was at most sessions to ensure every exercise was done precisely, and I can't thank him enough for his involvement. I'm not sure I could have played again without his help.

Towards the end of the season Dr Gilmour said I could bowl gently in the nets, and slowly build up to around medium pace. I sent down just a few overs off a short run and felt none the worse for it. Slowly, slowly, and with the instruction to stop immediately if I felt any pain, I built up to almost three-quarter pace by the end of the season. However, I realised that if I couldn't bowl at express pace again, I had to concentrate on

the finer points of fast bowling, like swinging the ball and making it move off the wicket.

One doctor doubted I'd ever be able to bowl at the top level again, but Frank Pyke and Dr Gilmour encouraged me and gave me confidence. If it hadn't been for the success I'd already tasted playing for Australia, I'm not sure I would have had the incentive to work so hard to return.

Although I was still bowling within my more limited capacity, as per doctor's orders, I was building up my speed. I got called up for a Shield game against South Australia, and as the Poms had arrived to contest the 1974–75 Ashes, the media began to speculate about my possible return. I noticed a few of the English players walk over to watch me in the nets, and they moved along quickly enough, figuring that this new-look Dennis Lillee wasn't going to trouble them. The press weren't that impressed either, but I got recalled to the team for the first Test in Brisbane.

It wasn't until I was three or four Tests into my return that I began to think it was really possible – that it was actually happening. It wasn't just my bowling action that had changed in this time, but my whole attitude. I realised that playing cricket for Australia was something that could be snatched away from me at any time, so I'd better start enjoying myself. ◓

TOP: Treating my back before going on a tour of the Windies. At this stage it was thought to be a muscular or joint problem. Stress fractures were discovered not long into the tour.

BOTTOM: As I was the first Test cricketer diagnosed with stress fractures of the spine, treatment was still a bit of an experiment. The recommended fix was to stay immobile as much as possible, spend six weeks in a cast then few months in a brace. These were incredibly difficult times for me, and I was told that I would probably never bowl again.

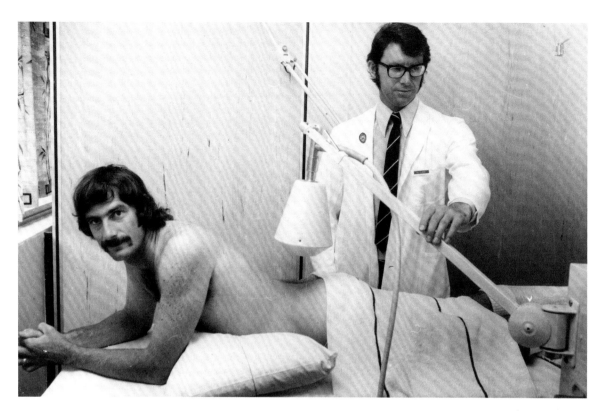

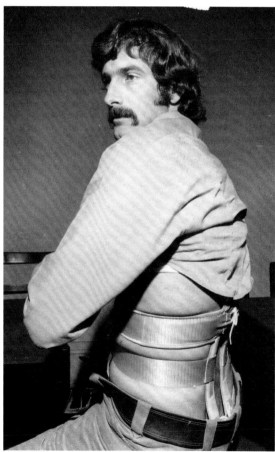

I recommend that all budding fast bowlers learn a good running technique early in their careers. I doubt I would have been able to come back from injury – and certainly not for as long as I did – if it hadn't been for the help of Austin Robertson Sr (pictured here). He was an Aussie Rules football great and held the world record for running over 140 yards (a record that stood for about 30 years). I was extremely lucky to have him as my running coach. He helped me remodel my whole running style, which meant I could bowl more effectively and efficiently, and without the same toll on my body. In 1972 his son, Austin Robertson Jr, also became my manager.

I loved running, and I probably ran just about every day after these photographs were taken in the early 1970s up until the time I was compiling this book. Sadly, my doctor recently told me that my knee was buggered and that I'd have to give up running.

WITH A LITTLE HELP FROM RICHIE BENAUD

I THOUGHT THESE MIGHT BE INTERESTING TO include, because they put what came later between myself and cricket authorities into some context, and also help to underline what an absolute legend Richie Benaud was.

This gives you a sense of what it was like for 25-year-old me back then. I had managed to play 11 Tests and then broken down with a career-threatening injury while playing for Australia. I couldn't afford the medical bills that were being sent, but the Australian Cricket Board (as it was called back then) was refusing to help out. Dr Gilmour was fantastic, by the way; he understood the situation and never once compromised on the quality of my treatment even though the bills weren't getting paid!

I didn't know what to do, or how to get myself out of the situation. I had focused on doing everything I could to get through the injury and, after 18 months, I was just about ready to play again. As you can see, I turned to Richie for help, and he took the time to guide me through my dealings with the board, which was a very intimidating thing for a young cricketer. Richie was unique in that he was loved and respected by all, and I dare say he smoothed the way for many successful careers and cricketing relationships over the years.

I'm not sure if I sought Richie's opinion on this, or if it was all impulse, but in a bold move, a week before the team for the first Test in the 1974–75 Ashes was to be announced I called the secretary of the Australian Cricket Board. I told him that if they were thinking about selecting me, they should think again because my medical bills had not been paid as promised. He said they had been, but I knew they hadn't because I checked before the call. I also said that if I was selected, I'd have no hesitation in explaining to the press why I couldn't play. I was that annoyed; it wasn't a lot of money for the board, but it certainly was to me.

Fortunately they blinked first, because I'm not sure how things would have gone otherwise. In the end I think it paid off for Australian cricket, because not only was I back, but it was the start of my partnership with one Jeff Thomson.

23rd July, 1974.

Mr. D. Lillee,
33 Nottingham Street,
EAST VIC PARK.....6101

Dear Mr. Lillee,

As you are probably aware, your account has now been outstanding for seven months. Would you please advise us when we may expect settlement of same.

Yours faithfully,

W. N. Gilmour
per M.

ABOVE: I found this in the files; it is a letter to the chairman of selectors for WA to tell him I wouldn't be accepting the position of vice-captain of WA.

Dear Dennis,

It seems a typical Board letter, though it is apparent that it is the Insurance Company that has told the Board that it (the Company) does not feel responsible for any more bills as you are bowling again.

As I recall it, your doctor, or rather the Board's doctor, indicated that bowling would do no harm so long as you took it easy and reported to him if there were any problems.

I would suggest a letter along the following lines:

Dear Alan,

I was sorry to receive your letter on behalf of the Australian Cricket Board stating that the Board will not pay any medical accounts concerning the back injury I sustained or aggravated on the West Indies tour.

As far as I am concerned, my main aim is to be fit for next season when England come here so that I can, hopefully, regain my place in the Board's Australian XI.

To that end I have had my back in plaster, had the plaster removed, have gone through gentle and more strenuous exercises and have played cricket at club level, first as a batsman/fieldsman/captain and then added not too strenuous bowling to the list.

The bowling was okayed by Dr. Gilmour by telephone between the October 18th X-rays and the December appointment, on the basis that "I could bowl as long as I take it easy and, if there is any pain, I should stop bowling and go and see him".

Mr. D.K. Lillee
Page Two
23rd February 1974

I have followed that advice as part of the treatment and, in fact, have suffered no pain, a fact which is very pleasing to me, and I'm sure will be to the Board as well, as they were the ones who instigated the medical treatment. I hope the same situation will apply to the end of the current Perth season and through the winter months when I will be continuing to follow the medical advice.

However, as I understand your letter, the Board has washed its hands of anything to do with my injury because, in some way, the Insurance cover has run out.

Does this mean that any further checkups I have are to be at my own expense and that the Board and Dr. Gilmour will no longer be in contact on the matter?

Could you also give me some guidance on what happens when next season begins. Would the Board or the selectors insist that I undergo more X-rays and at whose expense would these be?

I'm sorry the board feels that it can no longer pay for any further treatment for an injury sustained on tour but I would be grateful if you could help me with the queries I have listed.

Look forward to seeing you in Sydney for the game against N.S.W. and the 4th Test.

Kindest regards,

DENNIS

D.K. Lillee

Hope the above will help. Daph sends regards to you and Helen and hope all is well with you both.

Kindest regards,

Yours sincerely,

Richie Benaud

Not only was Richie reassuring, he gave me great advice on how to deal with the board.

The will to recover

Being interested in sport all my life, I first heard of Dennis in the early 1970s, and noted his incredible fighting spirit. He was so reliable: chants of 'Lillee, Lillee, Lillee,' would send shivers up the spines of the Poms and, inevitably, an important wicket would fall.

My introduction to sports medicine was when I dislocated my shoulder playing for South Sydney's first grade rugby league team and was referred to the NRL doctor – who was a gynaecologist. This was the state of treating sport injuries in Australia. There were no team doctors in the days when Dennis was injured; there were none of the major payments that the sport stars get today, and training had to fit around work.

I finished orthopaedic training in 1972 and immediately went to work at the Hughston Clinic in Columbus (Georgia, USA) to study sports medicine, as it wasn't recognised in Australia. They were just forming the American Orthopaedic Society for Sports Medicine. I was asked to join and have since devoted myself to the injured athlete.

I was honoured when the opportunity came up to treat Dennis. I already knew about his back, and that not many could recover completely from such an injury. When he came to see me I was using the arthroscope for knee injuries. It was necessary to operate on his right knee.

I analysed his style, particularly his landing on the right foot, and realised how his injury had occurred. As he landed, his right foot rotated inward, thus causing a shearing force in his knee, damaging the cartilage and locking his knee. This became a common injury in fast bowlers.

He obeyed strict postoperative advice and made a remarkable recovery. He was extremely intelligent and understood what was happening in his body, which helped him to recover. I also operated on his elbow and, many years later, we needed to 'adjust' his right knee again. He applied all his 'killer instinct' to his recovery. I asked him once why Greg Norman didn't have the same 'killer instinct', and Dennis joked that he was from Queensland and possibly had spent too much time on the beach.

Dennis and I have become friends. He has all the markings of a legend to me: humility, thoroughness and a willingness to help young cricketers.

Dr Mervyn Cross OAM, orthopaedic surgeon

This was the beginning of problems with my right knee, which have plagued me ever since. A top mate, and in my opinion the best knee doctor around, Merv Cross OAM, kept me on the field for many years.

Mad dogs and Englishmen – or just plain bravery? In 1974 Colin Cowdrey, at 41 years of age, faced Thommo and me in our primes on what was then the world's fastest wicket: the WACA.

5

FIRING UP

When I came back from injury I had a different mindset as well as a more refined action. While I had lost a bit of pace, I knew I had to bowl smarter. And with a new lease on my cricket life, I was determined to enjoy it.

This was a photo set-up with Thommo and me in the UK in 1975. It's amazing when our actions are frozen at the point of delivery – they are almost identical.

'Fixing up' DK

When I first played against Dennis, I was with New South Wales and went to Perth to show him what fast bowling was all about. I knew he liked to dominate. You get sportsmen that have big egos, and I don't mean it in a derogatory way but he was one of those. He had that self-belief – always thought he was going to do something special – and that's what made him the bowler he was.

He came out on this day acting like he owned the place, and I just thought, 'I'll fix you up.' My second ball to him was short and knocked the bat out of his hand. Dennis didn't say a word. He was gobsmacked. He wasn't used to that, especially from a new bloke. He didn't know who the hell I was. I just did that to everyone, and he wasn't going to get any special treatment.

The ball flew off to gully but it was never going to get to the boundary. I was distracted by the sight of Kerry O'Keeffe and Dougie Walters trying to catch the thing. It was a bloody comedy. Then I looked up and saw that Dennis was at my end, and he just said, 'I hope you can fucking bat, pal.'

'Have you lost your bat, mate?' I said. 'There it is, up the other end. Why don't you shut your mouth and go pick it up. I saw you bowl this morning and you were shit, and now I see you can't bat for shit. I guess that makes you a pretty even all-rounder!' He just stood there, looking at me with an expression that said, *Who is this cockhead?*

Dougie Walters rushed over and said, 'Don't you know who that is? That's Dennis Lillee. He'll kill the fucking lot of us.'

'Why don't you shut up as well, Dougie?' I said. 'You're all a pack of gutless pricks. Why don't you come out with the same attitude as Ronnie?' (That was Ronnie Crippin, who liked to take on fast bowling and made about 80 in our innings.) For good measure, I turned back to Dennis and yelled, 'Look at him, he looks like a fucking clown as well.' Dennis just stood there, without saying a word.

Gary Gilmour and I eventually bowled them out, and then it was our second innings. Dennis absolutely went through us, taking something like six for shit, and the match was over in two and a half days. I should have shut up.

That's just the way it was where I was from, and the people I grew up playing cricket with – like Lennie Pascoe – were the same. Dennis knew I wasn't going to back off from anyone, and I think he looked forward to that when we got to open together for Australia. He was the enforcer, the guy getting in the face of the batsmen.

I used to go harder on myself than anything. He'd be bowling off cutters and that sort of thing, and I just tried to bowl really quick and scare the shit out of the batsmen. It was a great attack because we'd go hard for the opening spell, get a couple of wickets each, and then you'd have someone like Gary Gilmour, a really good swing bowler, come in. He'd get one, they'd be five-down and in trouble, and then we'd come back to finish them off.

Jeff Thomson, 51 Tests for Australia

TEAMING UP WITH THOMMO

MY FIRST GAME WITH JEFF THOMSON WAS eminently forgettable. It was against Pakistan early in the 1972–73 season. I was battling the back injury that would soon sideline me when selectors took the plunge and gave Thommo, the young firebrand from Bankstown with an unusual slinging action, his first baggy green.

What would become a lethal combination almost backfired from the start, because we were far from impressive: I took 1–90 and 2–59 with Thommo's return being 0–100 and 0–10. It was only revealed later that he was bowling with a broken bone in his foot, which he hadn't mentioned for fear of missing his chance.

But there was nothing quiet about Thommo once he got going again in the Sheffield Shield, with rival batsmen around the country nursing bruises and broken

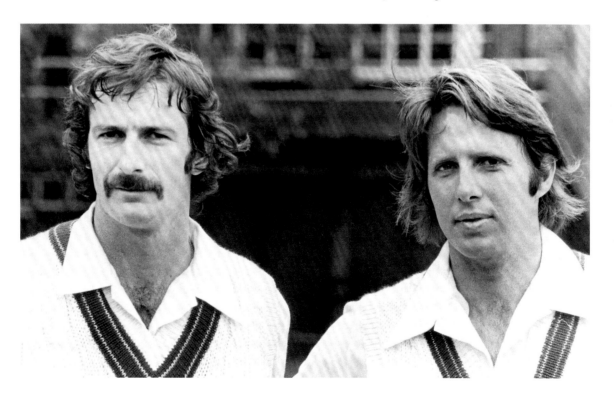

Thommo and I formed an opening partnership for Australia that was built around pace. It lasted many years and was great fun, as he's a great mate as well.

The 1974–75 Ashes team. Back row (L–R): Doug Walters; Jeff Thomson; me; Max Walker; Ashley Mallett; Rick McCosker; Terry Jenner. Front row (L–R): Rod Marsh; Ian Redpath; Ian Chappell; Ross Edwards; Greg Chappell.

bones as he vented his fury. By the time the first Test against Mike Denness's England came around in 1974–75, the temptation to give Thommo another try was irresistible.

By then I was hopeful that my back problems were behind me (no pun intended), and the prospect of sharing the new ball with someone as fast and exciting as Thommo was tantalising.

I bumped into him in the Queensland Cricketers' Club at the Gabba the night before the first Test – his big chance to really show what he could do. I complimented him on drinking water on the eve of such a big occasion, and Thommo casually informed me that it was heavily laced with Scotch. He always seemed to bowl better, he told me, when he was feeling a bit 'fuzzy'.

I went to bed that night wondering just how it was all going to pan out. I needn't have worried; by the end of that Test all had been revealed as 'fuzzy' Thommo scared the living daylights out of the Poms to finish with 3–59 and 6–46 in a 166-run victory. On my return I got two scalps in each innings, and so the pair of us relaunched our partnership with 13 of England's 20 wickets to fall. ●

THE BOUNCER WAR

THAT FIRST TEST AGAINST ENGLAND IN THE 1974–75 season was also memorable because England's all-rounder Tony Greig inadvertently started what was to become a bouncer war.

When I walked out to bat I overheard Greig telling paceman Peter Lever to serve me up a few short-pitched deliveries. But Lever must have been feeling tired or was honouring the 'fast bowlers pact', and so Greig was brought into the attack and immediately slipped a couple of bouncers into me. When I tried to hook the second one I got an edge, and Alan Knott took the catch. I bristled as I walked off the ground, leaned in to Greig and said, 'Just remember who started this.' He just chuckled, and he had the last laugh, too.

When he came out to bat we peppered him alright, but he just stood back and slashed his way to 110 – the first Englishman to score a century at the Gabba since 1936–37. He really wound us up that day and showed a lot of arrogance by signalling boundaries himself. I knew then it was going to be on for young and old.

Results of a bouncer to me from Tony Greig – the one that started it all.

Things intensified. When England suffered a couple of injuries, they flew in Colin Cowdrey from the middle of an English winter for the second Test in Perth. He was just a few days short of his 42nd birthday and hadn't played Test cricket since June 1971. We all thought it was a joke, but the old bloke showed plenty of guts under pressure with scores of 22 at first drop and 41 when he opened the second innings.

But England needed more than Cowdrey to keep Thomson at bay, and he finished with 2–45 and 5–93. Australia won by nine wickets, with a highlight being Doug Walters hooking Bob Willis for six to bring up a century off the last ball of the day.

As the new-ball hostilities continued, with Thomson taking eight wickets and myself four in the drawn third Test at the MCG, the story goes that England opener David Lloyd wrote a letter home to his mother: 'Mum, things are looking up, today I got a half-volley in the nets.'

By the time we got to Sydney for the fourth Test, Denness, the England Captain, had dropped himself from the team after making only 65 runs from six innings. Greig fired things up again when he hit me on the arm with yet another short one, and I came out breathing fire. But, I have to admit, I was particularly concerned when I forced John Edrich from the field after hitting him

ABOVE: In his last 12 months before this series, Dennis Amiss had amassed a world-record number of Test runs. On this tour, though, he couldn't take a trick. He just kept finding ways to get out to me.

OPPOSITE: After our confrontation earlier, Greig took the long handle to Thommo and me, combining skill and luck to make a hundred. Once Thommo discovered that the yorker – or 'sandshoe crusher', as he named it – was the delivery that the giant of a man found most difficult to play, Greigy struggled.

in the ribs with the first ball I bowled to him. Showing typical courage, he came back, hung in and nearly saved the game for England. But our 171-run win gave Australia back the Ashes. We partied long and hard that night.

We got to Adelaide, where I took four wickets in each innings, but Thommo injured a shoulder playing social tennis on the rest day and took no further part in the series. Down 0–4 in the series, England headed for the sixth Test in Melbourne, salivating at the prospect of not having to face Thomson. To their delight, I'm sure, I only bowled a few overs in that Test before having to sit out the match with a burst bursa in my right foot that required surgery. Suddenly our opening attack, which had so demoralised England, was no more.

To say England cashed in is an understatement. Denness bounced back with 188 and Keith Fletcher scored 146 as England won by an innings and four runs. Such a heavy defeat took a bit of the gloss off our summer, but with my back in great shape, both Thommo and I felt pleased with ourselves after taking 58 wickets between us. ●

This was a blow to Edrich's ribs that brought him to his knees. He left the field to have X-rays and it was discovered that his ribs were broken. It's a testament to the gutsy player he was that he returned later in England's innings and, in the face of much pain, played extremely well. Despite Edrich being a tough opponent, I have nothing but admiration for him.

Downtime in Hong Kong in 1974. Rod Marsh and I were on a promotional trip for the Hong Kong Cricket Club. The interesting part was when they set up a net in the ballroom of the Excelsior Hotel where Rod and I coached all comers!

Coming back better

As a wicketkeeper, it's a very natural thing to have a close working relationship with the bowlers in the team. When you have a match-winning bowler, it's even more important!

When I first saw Dennis bowl I wasn't 100 per cent convinced he was going to be a great first-class bowler. Sure, he was quick, but he was also wild. There were a few other fast bowlers in club cricket in Perth who were almost as quick and probably had more refined actions.

It wasn't until I actually played with him that I realised we had something special. His attitude was just superb. He wanted to learn, he wanted to succeed, but more than anything he wanted to bowl. His everlasting theory was, 'If you bowl half the overs then you should finish up with half the wickets.' This equated to five per innings, 10 per match!

It was a devil of a struggle to get the ball from DK when he was bowling. He always wanted another over. He got himself involved in the contest and, as far as he was concerned, there was only ever going to be one winner. Somehow you had to make him think it was time for him to have a spell. This, of course, wasn't easy.

Because we were such different people, when we first played together we didn't spend a whole heap of time together. I loved playing golf and having a few beers, whereas DK enjoyed shopping and sleeping, so we didn't see much of each other on days off.

When we both became regular members of the Australian team it was only natural that we would become much closer friends. We spent hours upon hours travelling together from one side of Australia to the other, and more often than not we sat together. We talked a lot of cricket and a lot about the different batsmen we were to play against. I guess this is where we did most of our planning, and where we developed a really good understanding of each other.

Dennis had his share of injuries but was always able to find a way of getting himself back into the game. Funnily enough, he seemed to come back a better bowler each time. I put this down to the amount of work he did on his body to be able to cope with the rigours of fast bowling. He was never first to training but he was always last to leave. After a decent net session, when the rest of us decided a cold beer was the way to go, Dennis would opt for another 20 sprints.

As the seasons came and went, DK and I became even closer pals. We finished up rooming together on interstate and overseas tours and, if anything, our friendship has continued to grow, even though it's more than 30 years since we played together. I suppose we should sit in the Lillee–Marsh Stand and have a decent bottle of red together, but that's not our style. We're naturally proud to have a stand named after us, but we also realise it'll be bowled over one day.

In the meantime, to quote Dennis, 'We might as well start enjoying ourselves.'

Rod Marsh, 96 Tests for Australia

I love this shot, which shows the pace and poise of a fast bowler. It could be any one of us, anywhere.

So much for a quiet night

After our classic prank on him during the Australia A tour of New Zealand in 1970, Dennis went from being the most gullible on the team to the most skeptical. He wouldn't believe anything unless he actually saw it written down.

He was always on guard, although I do remember another 'unfortunate' incident a few years later in Adelaide, on the night before we had a Test match against Pakistan. The forecast was for sweltering heat for the next few days, which was going to be hard for everyone – and particularly the fast bowlers. Dinner finished at 8.30pm, and Dennis announced that he was heading off to bed.

'What are you talking about?' I said.

'I need to sleep.'

'How much sleep do you need?'

'Eight hours.'

'Well, if you go to bed now you'll be up in the middle of the night thinking about the cricket too much. Come and have a drink with us.'

'Nah, I want to go bed.'

'Listen, mate, there is no chance you'll be bowling tomorrow. If I win the toss, we'll bat. If they win, they'll send us in because they won't want to face you and Thommo on the first day. Let's go down to the hotel and have a drink with the rest of the team. I'll have you back in bed by 11pm. Promise.'

He finally relented, and we all went out for a drink. At 11pm, on the dot, he tapped me on the shoulder and said, 'Let's go back.'

'Take it easy, Dennis, we're having a good time. And you won't be bowling tomorrow!' I persuaded him to stay for one more hour. Anyway, we got home shortly after midnight – quite a bit after midnight, actually.

Traditionally I never looked at the pitch before the day of play, because I didn't want to make my decision based on what I thought the wicket *might* be like but instead what it actually *was* like. We got to the ground the next day, and it was already stinking hot. When I got out there, there was a green sheen on the wicket, and the curator had obviously left quite a bit of moisture on it given the forecast. So I won the toss, and decided we'd bowl.

As I was walking off, I realised that I might have a problem with our main bowler. 'Sorry, boys, we're bowling,' I said casually when I entered the dressing room. They all assumed we'd lost the toss, and I didn't feel the need to correct them. Dennis got on with it.

He started bowling from the northern end and I was fielding, looking back towards the scoreboard, when I realised that the scoreboard said that Australia won the toss. Nothing happened for the first four balls, but then Dennis happened to glance up at the scoreboard and noticed who'd won the toss. He just about flipped his lid. At the top of his mark – I can't repeat all of it – but he started yelling, 'You rotten bastard …!'

Nobody else knew what was going on. It just looked like Dennis had flipped out in the middle of an over. And the first over at that! Rod Marsh turned to me and said, 'What's wrong with him?'

I just shrugged. 'No idea.' Then, on the next ball, Dennis followed through about 23 yards past the wicket and started abusing me. 'You rotten bastard, you said we weren't bowling today!' And on, and on.

Anyway, we bowled them out in 70 overs. 'There you go,' I said, 'you can have your rest now.'

He really was brilliant, and I've never known anyone to be fitter and more dedicated to conditioning than Dennis. Few would have been able to come back from the injuries he suffered physically, never mind mentally. The strength it took for him to get through six weeks in a cast, virtually with a broken back, I can't even imagine. People thought if he came back, he'd be a medium pacer at best, but he went on to become one of the greatest fast bowlers of all time.

Greg Chappell, former captain of Australia, 87 Tests

Walking back to my mark was a good time to reflect on the last delivery and get my mind and body ready to decide what type of delivery to bowl next. Or, in the case Greg is referring to here, to check the scoreboard and catch him out lying!

THE FIRST WORLD CUP

THE INAUGURAL 1975 WORLD CUP LAUNCHED one of the game's truly great competitions, but it's memorable to me for the incredible effort of my teammate Gary Gilmour and the arrival of a most formidable foe in Isaac Vivian Alexander Richards.

We would never have reached the final without Gary. The semifinal against England was played at Headingley, and we expected a tough game facing the most experienced one-day players in the world. We bowled on a green top, and Gary was almost unplayable, finishing with 6–14 from 12 overs as England was bundled out for 93. He then rescued

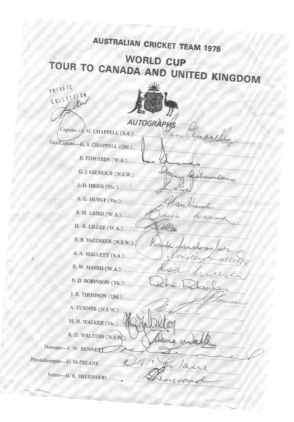

us with the bat as well, going to the wicket with Australia 6–39 and top-scoring with 28 not out.

We had met Viv Richards as a brash 20-year-old during a tour match two years earlier in the game against the Leeward Islands in Antigua. It was before my back injury stopped me, and I had him caught on five by Ian Chappell in the slips. He didn't bat in the second innings, and we didn't think anything more of him.

In a qualifying game at The Oval, he batted down the order and scored 15 not out, while Gary Gilmour bowled him for five in the final when he came out at number six. But it was his fielding that made the difference in that final. He ran out three Australians including three of our top four batsmen. It was a trait of his game that never diminished.

Viv must be rated as one of, if not *the*, best fieldsmen of all time. With a bat in his hand, when he got into his groove, I rate him the best I ever bowled to.

In the final, we were chasing 291 from 60 overs, after Clive Lloyd led the damage with 102. Our ninth wicket fell at 233, but Jeff Thomson and I still thought we had a chance. Not so the thousands of West Indies fans who'd lined the boundary. Or, for that matter, our teammates, who were busy packing their kits to get back to the hotel.

As Thommo and I inched closer, the players' balcony suddenly filled up. When Thommo hit a catch to Roy Fredericks at mid-off, the fans

rubbish bin lids – to belt out some celebratory music. It was great to be part of the first of what would become a very prestigious event.

I must say, though, I'm not a fan of the way the World Cup is structured these days. While I've never been one to stand in the way of progress, I think the competition has been diminished by the expansion to 14 teams.

The inclusion of 'minnows' makes the tournament too long and reduces its once significant credibility. None of these teams are going to win the World Cup in the near future, and there are plenty of tournaments, such as T20 events, in which they can compete.

I recommend that each of the minnows be rated every year according to their successes against the top teams. The two or three teams that rate the highest should be included in the World Cup every four years, which would make for a better competition for everyone.

Each World Cup would produce different teams from the minnow pool until eventually their consistent performance would enable them to become a full member of the top echelon of World Cup participants. People may say that this won't help those countries develop, but I feel that being consistently smashed by top teams can do more lasting damage. Earning their stripes during the lead-up to the World Cup would help the team, and individuals within it, to believe. Success would inevitably follow. ●

charged onto the ground. Fredericks heard the umpire's 'no ball' call and shied at the bowler's end stumps to get rid of me, but he missed and the ball disappeared into the stampeding fans. Thommo and I just kept running up and down the wicket until the umpire stopped us, eventually only letting us have two runs. We still needed 18 from a dozen or so balls, but Thommo lurched well down the wicket and was run out when Deryck Murray underarmed the ball into the stumps.

The West Indies fans grabbed anything they could get hold of – from beer cans to

ABOVE: Alvin Kallicharran was on fire, hooking me for six at The Oval in 1975 during a World Cup qualifier. He was always a stumbling block for us when we played against the West Indies.

OPPOSITE: The bane of touring was signing team sheets. We must have signed around 20,000 sheets during a tour of the UK. They seemed to fill up all of our spare time and followed us everywhere we went.

An auspicious occasion. Queen Elizabeth II, Prince Philip and Prince Charles with international cricketers set to compete in the inaugural Cricket World Cup, outside Buckingham Palace, London, June 1975. To avoid losing HRH in the fold of this page, we had to cut a few heads off at the edges. Sorry chaps!

Letting one go against England in Headingley, 1975.

ON 'SAFARI' WITH DAD FOR THE 1975 ASHES

DURING THE 1975 ASHES TOUR MY OLD MAN, who had barely even left Perth before, suddenly turned up unannounced in the dressing room at Lord's. Dad had sworn one of my teammates to secrecy after calling him at the hotel and arranging for a ticket into the ground and inner sanctum.

That was the only thing quiet about his arrival, as he was wearing a purple safari suit that made him stand out like a beacon. He stayed for the remainder of the tour and was feted wherever he went. After a couple of months of him following us around, some of the players in the Australian team very impolitely pointed out to him that the buttons on his safari suit didn't quite do up anymore.

Mike Denness had retained the England captaincy, despite his wretched tour of Australia. But at the first Test, at Edgbaston,

I didn't know Dad was coming to the UK and was I shocked and delighted. He had never even been on a plane before!

his decision to send Australia in (the first time an England captain had ever made such a decision at that venue) was the last straw for the selectors, and he soon lost the captaincy.

We rattled up 359, Rod Marsh top-scoring with 61. When England were one over into their chase, the heavens opened up and flooded the uncovered wicket (those were the days of uncovered pitches). We took full advantage, with myself taking 5–15 and Max Walker 5–48 as England was bundled out for 101. They were forced to follow on. Thommo ran through them with five wickets for 38 runs. We won by an innings and 85 runs.

Tony Greig was appointed skipper for the second Test at Lord's, and I wondered if his aggressive attitude in the field would flow though into his captaincy. It didn't really emerge, but his strong competitive spirit certainly lifted his players. Tony led by example and top-scored with 96. England had slumped to 4–49. Thommo was a bit askew with 28 no balls and six wides, and Ross Edwards joined the heartbreak club with 99 in our first innings.

> Dad's presence must have fired me up because I went out and made my highest first-class score of 73 not out from 103 deliveries, with three sixes and eight fours. It was easy to find the purple safari suit as I held my bat up to him upon reaching 50.

This photo emphasises my follow-through, which is essential to bowl fast and swing a ball.

Another century nipped in the bud! Not a classical shot, but effective on my way to my best Test score of 73 not out, here at Lord's in 1975. My Dad, Keith, had come to the UK to see some cricket, but I bet he didn't expect this!

The third Test at Headingley was drawn when vandals badly damaged one end of the pitch after play on the fourth day (they were protesting against the jailing of a robber named George Davis). The big loser was opener Rick McCosker. He was left stranded five runs short of his maiden Test century, but he got his just desserts in the final Test at The Oval with 127, while Ian Chappell hit 192. It ended in a draw, but the Edgbaston victory was enough for us to win the series.

I have many fond memories of that tour – including my 21 wickets – but I especially enjoyed sharing the time with my dad and a great bunch of blokes.

RIGHT: I've kept a few cartoons from down the years, and this is one of my favourites.

Dennis Amiss again. Note the extremely aggressive field placements. There are all 11 of the Aussie players behind the wickets at Amiss's end, including me, the bowler and the fine leg (who can't be seen).

Alan Hurst, Bruce Laird and me window-shopping in London, 1975.

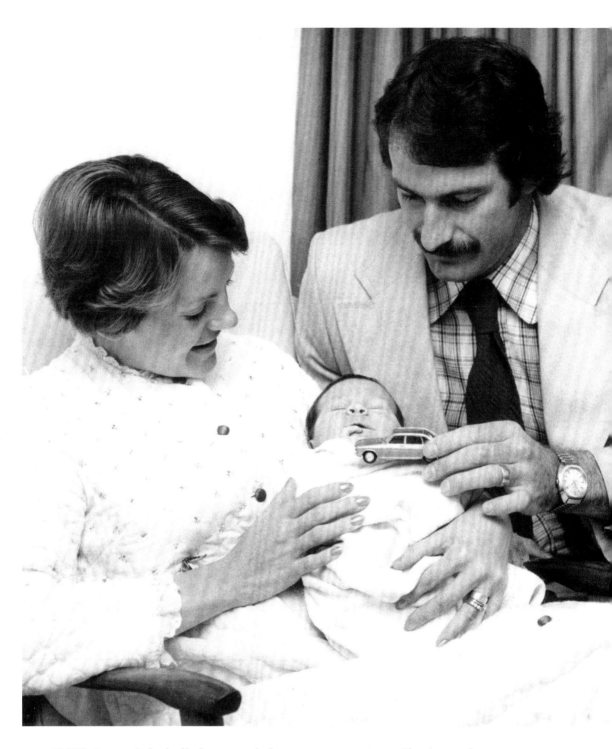

ABOVE: I was at the birth of both my sons, which were amazing experiences. This photo is of our youngest, Dean. I brought in a toy car for him and, although he might not have appreciated it at the time, cars are now one of his great passions.

OPPOSITE TOP: Our firstborn, Adam, with his proud parents.

OPPOSITE BOTTOM: Adam, our eldest, was introduced to cricket at a tender age.

AGAINST THE WEST INDIES

AUSTRALIA'S STUNNING 5–1 SERIES SUCCESS AGAINST the West Indies in the summer of 1975–76 proved to be a false horizon considering what Clive Lloyd's men inflicted on world cricket over much of the next decade.

Having been beaten in the World Cup final only a few months beforehand, we expected a tough series – which it seemingly was at 1–1 after the Brisbane and Perth Tests. We were annihilated at the WACA by an innings and 87 runs. My theory is that they were keen observers of the previous season when England went down 4–1 to Australia after playing pretty tentative cricket.

That certainly wasn't the way Lloyd's men were going to play it, but I reckon their all-out aggression ultimately undid them. They could not sustain the effort for the whole series, going down by pretty big margins in the remaining four Tests. When the dust had settled, 29 of those wickets had gone to Jeff Thomson, 27 to myself and 20 to Gary Gilmour.

Australia had a superb batting list, and the West Indies attack had not yet peaked. Malcolm Marshall, Colin Croft and Joel Garner had not burst onto the scene yet, but when they did Lloyd knew he had an attack from which no batsman could hide.

Viv Richards, who opened in the last two Tests for scores of 30, 101, 50 and 98, is said to have been hypnotised by Dr Rudi Webster after totalling only 147 runs from his first seven digs. If so, what an outcome for him! And of course he continued that dominance shown in those last two Tests for the rest of a great career.

Gordon Greenidge was used only twice, with a pair on debut in the first Test and three and eight in the third Test in Melbourne. Desmond Haynes and Larry Gomes hadn't arrived, but the Windies lost nothing there with Roy Fredericks and Alvin Kallicharran.

> While Lloyd and his men, when finally fully operational, went on to inflict much pain and plunge Australia into the depths of despair many times, at least the home team got to enjoy some highs in this series.

In Brisbane Greg Chappell became the first captain to score centuries in each innings of his first Test in command, and I quietly savoured my 100th scalp in my 22nd Test: that of 'Smokin' Joe'. Chappell's twin centuries showed just how determined he was to lead by example, a trait he would have picked up from his elder brother.

Despite Australia losing heavily in Perth, at least Ian Chappell, with scores of 156 and

(continued on page 108)

The great Viv Richards in action, 1976.

Cut from the same cloth

Dennis and I had some epic battles over the years. I've been the recipient of his bouncers, having them go past my head at around 100 miles per hour. After each bouncer would come the famous glare, and maybe some choice words to let you know there was another one coming and it would be even faster than the last. I admit that he got a few words and glares back too, which made our battles all the more intriguing. That was only on the field though; off the field we've always been very relaxed together.

I have always respected Dennis as one of the best fast bowlers I have ever faced. He was quick, accurate and consistent. In addition to his obvious talents and skills as a bowler, he was a fierce competitor and had a tremendous will to win. The quality of his bowling at the end of the day, even at times when he had been toiling, was the same as when he started. He always dug deeper to bowl with the same energy and give his all. We were both cut from the same cloth in that we took great pride in representing our regions, and losing or failure just weren't in our lexicons.

Sir Viv Richards, 121 Tests for the West Indies

20, became the fourth Australian after Don Bradman, Neil Harvey and Bill Lawry to reach 5000 in Test cricket. He set another record in the third Test in Melbourne, becoming the first Australian to hold 100 catches in Tests when he snapped up Lawrence Rowe. As with Rod Marsh, I cannot remember Ian Chappell ever dropping a catch off my bowling.

> Everyone drops catches, but when Rod and Ian put one down in the slips cordon it must have been off someone else; I just can't recall them letting me down.

Greg Chappell was also a mighty fine slips fieldsman, and I have always believed the pair's unique catching style reflected their batting. Greg was a very elegant batsman and that's exactly how I saw his style in the slips. Ian was more spectacular at the crease and, to me, that's how he fielded too – he would throw himself all over the place.

Ian was at the centre of an unusual incident during that fourth Test when the tourists launched a deafening appeal for a catch from the first delivery Michael Holding bowled to him. Chappell, as he always did, stood his ground and waited for the umpire to make the decision. When the umpire ruled in favour of the batsman, the young Jamaican, playing in only his third Test, walked back to the top of his mark and sat down either in protest or disappointment, or both.

Skipper Lloyd, fielding in the slips, didn't move a muscle. I guess it was Lloyd's way of saying, 'If you want to play Test cricket under me, you had better work it out yourself.' Eventually Holding got back to work and, to his credit, had Chappell caught behind with only four runs to his name.

Then in the fifth Test at the Adelaide Oval, something equally unusual happened. The dour but highly effective opener Ian Redpath, playing his 117th innings in his 65th Test, belted the only two sixes of his Test career.

Redpath valued his wicket like no one I knew, rigidly adhering to the Don Bradman principle of keeping the ball on the ground. I wondered if 'Redders' was taking up a challenge from someone or whether, because he was nearing the end of his career, he wanted to add something new to his already impressive CV.

Redpath, who scored 103 and 65 in that Test, followed with 101 and 70 as Australia rounded out a spectacular series with a 165-run win at the MCG. Lloyd and the West Indies went home licking their wounds, but it wouldn't be long before they regrouped to wreak havoc on an unprecedented scale. ●

TOP: A motley impromptu band, led by one of my heroes, Wes Hall. L–R: me; Bob Massie; Wes Hall; Jeff Hammond.

BOTTOM: Sir Gary Sobers was always welcome in our dressing rooms. Doug Walters, typically, is minding the beer glasses while I'm on Coca Cola.

Camaraderie among cricketers

The first time I ever faced Dennis Lillee was in Jamaica, when I was about 19 and batting at around 10 or 11. I tell you, I didn't even see the ball and had no idea where it was. I just remember that suddenly my legs went numb, and it turned out the ball was jammed between them. It wasn't until I took a step and the ball dropped that I saw it. I swear he could have killed me that day because I had absolutely no idea where the ball was.

A couple of years later, when I was 21, I was lucky enough to play for my country against the Australians on the 1975–76 tour. My fondest memories from that tour were sitting in the dressing rooms after matches and listening in to the conversations between the likes of Dennis Lillee and Clive Lloyd, Ian Chappell and Lance Gibbs, Rod Marsh and Deryck Murray. I was too young to get involved in that sort of thing, but I loved it. There was fierce competition out

in the field but incredible camaraderie off it. They were the good old days; it didn't matter what happened on the field, you would always enjoy a beer together afterwards – or in my case back then, just a soft drink. You don't get that anymore: teams are aggressive off the field as well as on it.

I didn't try to be like Dennis because I was doing my own thing. But I remember admiring his rhythm and run-up, particularly the slow build-up of pace and trying to make sure that I was going at my fastest when I delivered the ball.

World Series Cricket was a fierce competition, the toughest I played in. Packer demanded results, and you had to be at your very best all the time. But as hard as the competition was, it was still social off the field and we used to see each other over breakfast and throughout the day. That was a jolly good time. World Series Cricket really helped us get better, and the West Indies came back to Australia in 1979–80 and beat Australia 2–0. That was just huge, and I still remember that celebration in Adelaide. World Series Cricket was one thing, but to represent your country and your people and take a historic win in Australia was just an unbelievably good feeling.

I remember in that series someone had hit Dennis Lillee on the finger. His finger was split and we knew he wouldn't want to not bowl. He tried to put tape on his finger, but Lloydy objected to him wearing the tape, and Dennis Lillee totally lost it. I can remember him coming into the dressing room and pleading with Lloydy, but Lloydy wasn't having any of it. You can't give a bowler that good any sort of leeway. So Dennis had to bowl without tape, and we knew the seam would have been burning his finger, and we liked that. But he still bowled alright. It just shows that the competition was fierce, no inch given, but like the tour before it there was still that same camaraderie between all the cricketers, win or lose. It's no coincidence that so many of us from those times are good friends now.

Would he have got a place in the famed West Indies pace attack of the late seventies? You could never question quality like that. It would have been Dennis Lillee and three others.

Michael Holding, 60 Tests for the West Indies

No one escaped a good bouncer – especially if they held us up too long while batting. Not even Lance Gibbs, who was a truly dedicated number 11 batsman. But whatever happened on the field, we were all mates afterwards.

With Compliments of

eurocars SOUTH PERTH AND CANNINGTON
Suppliers of
RENAULT—PEUGEOT VEHICLES, BICYCLES AND BOATS.

Working for a living

A couple of years after I had met Dennis socially I was shocked to read on the front page of the newspaper that he was 'Unemployed': he was unable to get work in Perth and was contemplating an offer from a Queensland-based radio station that was already employing his 'Speed Twin', Jeff Thompson. I got hold of Dennis and we arranged to meet first thing the next Monday morning.

Dennis explained that he was unable to hold down a regular job because of the time he needed to be away playing for his state and country.

In 1976 I offered him a position as promotions and advertising manager with Eurocars (the WA distributors for Renault and Peugeot), which came with a new car *and* all the time required to pursue his cricket career. He said he knew nothing about the automotive industry or the role of promotions and advertising manager, but I brushed aside his doubts and told him I'd teach him all he needed to know. And that was that.

Basically, when he wasn't away playing cricket, his job was to meet and greet clients as they visited our dealership, and to sign their logbooks when they took delivery of their new cars. Dennis took to the job with typical focus and before long he was the face of Eurocars. Employing him turned out to be the best business decision I'd ever made. With Dennis helping to entice customers, Eurocars became the most successful Renault showroom in the country.

At the Kalgoorlie Car Show, we were inundated by people requesting brochures signed by Dennis Lillee. The neighbouring Mitsubishi stand asked us if we were ever going to take Dennis for lunch so people might look at their cars. At the same show, Dennis had to maintain his training regime and asked if I'd pace him on a run. 'No,' he said, responding to the horror in my expression, 'you don't have to run, just drive the car and I'll run behind. When I start to drop off, turn back.' And so we did, for 12 miles.

Then he needed some bowling practice and took us to the Kalgoorlie Oval. He just handed me a bat and walked back to the crease, while another colleague, Barry, took up position behind the stumps.

I could see Dennis's arm rising, but not the ball. It would just thump the ground before me, rise over my head or whistle past my ear. I'm a former WA Rally champion but this was the most terrifying sporting moment of my life! Then I started to hear the familiar chant of 'Lillee, Lillee, Lillee'. I thought the fear must have been making me hallucinate but then I looked around to see hundreds of people glued to the cyclone fence, watching their idol bowl. They must have been thinking, *Who's the dummy with the bat missing five deliveries in every six?!* But I faced Lillee and survived to tell the tale.

Rod Slater, Dennis's old boss at Eurocars

Being the face of Eurocars, and promotions and advertising manager, was one of my most enjoyable expereinces in a workplace thanks to its owner, Rod Slater. He employed me when I found it almost impossible to hold down a job due to Test cricket commitments. Such enjoyable work.

ABOVE: Rod entertaining us all with a yarn on the This is Your Life *program dedicated to me.*

LEFT: This was a skit for an English newspaper ahead of the royal wedding between Diana and Charles.

Other jobs that never worked out ...

TOP: The beginning and end of my modelling career. Someone in the UK paid me to get dressed up in this clobber, and how could I say no?

CENTRE LEFT: This was a pilot for a sport quiz show, with me as the front man. It must have been woeful because I never heard from them again!

BOTTOM LEFT: Myself and Rod during a break from recording a sketch for the Paul Hogan Show in the 1970s.

BOTTOM RIGHT: DJ DK.

Combined teams for the Centenary Test in Melbourne, 1977. Back row (L–R): Amiss; Hookes; Woolmer; Gilmour; Lever; O'Keeffe; Willis; Cosier; Old; Robinson; Barlow; Bright; Davis; Randall. Front row(L–R): Fletcher; Walker; Knott; Marsh; Greig; Chappell; Brearley; Walters; Underwood; and yours truly.

THE CENTENARY TEST

MY MIND WAS ABUZZ WHEN I WALKED OUT TO bat on the first day of the Centenary Test against England in Melbourne. It was 12 March 1977, and Australia was in a spot of bother at 8–117. But although I was determined to help rescue the team, that was not at the forefront of my thoughts.

I gazed up at what appeared to be a capacity MCG crowd. I was struck by the privilege of being able to play in such a rare and prestigious match in front of so many people,

including dignitaries and former champion players. The Australian Cricket Board had assembled 218 of the 224 surviving Australia and England players for the occasion, and to rub shoulders with many of them before the Test had been very special. I was in awe. I half-expected WG Grace to walk through the door!

I was also acutely aware that I was part of something, which very few other people knew about, that would soon rock the

In the company of Sir Donald Bradman (centre) and former England bowler Harold Larwood (right) at a function before the Centenary Test, 1977. I doubt 'the Don' would have looked as relaxed if he'd known what was afoot with World Series Cricket.

cricket establishment to its foundations. Plans for World Series Cricket were afoot, and my involvement in Test cricket would soon be put in jeopardy. That was hard to take, especially on this occasion when I was so vividly reminded of how my boyhood dreams had become reality. But it was also, I believe, impossible to avoid.

Another thing that came to mind as I gazed up at this massive crowd was an idea I'd put forward some time before. In those days, with Australian players earning so little for their efforts (we were paid only $400 for playing in the Centenary Test, for example), and no such thing as a yearly contract, we cricketers were getting disillusioned and finding it increasingly difficult to balance playing elite cricket and earning a living.

My proposal was that every person who walked through the turnstiles, including members, paying adults and kids, pay an extra levy of 50 cents, which would go directly to the Australian players out in the middle. With a total of around 250,000 spectators having turned up to watch the Centenary Test, that would have meant that in this game alone each member of the Australian team – plus the 12th man – would have earned in excess of $10,000.

Not every Test would have reaped us that sort of reward, but whatever the amount it would surely have been better than the going rate at that time. But my suggestion fell on deaf ears, and the concept of World Series Cricket, which would give players a greater say, gathered momentum.

At the crease, I focused again and remained

unbeaten on 10 as Australia was bowled out for only 138. Unsurprisingly, our skipper, Greg Chappell, top-scored with 40, but all the attention was on opener Rick McCosker who, on four, had suffered a broken jaw and fallen on his wicket when struck by Bob Willis.

This scrupulously planned Test looked like being a real fizzer when England was bowled out for 95. Their skipper, Tony Greig, was also their top scorer, but with only 18. I guess I was partly to blame for that after collecting 6–26 off 13.3 overs, along with Max Walker who grabbed 4–54 off 15.

But after the halfway point, the match came alive. Ian Davis, with Kerry O'Keeffe as his opener in the absence of Rick, finished with 68, and Doug Walters contributed 66 as Australia pushed its lead well past 200. The departure of Ian brought debutante David Hookes to the crease. In one memorable over he pounded Tony to the fence off five successive deliveries on his way to 56.

Marsh was showing signs of becoming the first wicketkeeper to score a Test century, but was rapidly running out of partners.

Then one of the most remarkable things I've witnessed on a cricket field brought tears to my eyes. Rick, his head swathed in bandages, his face shockingly swollen with his jaw wired up, walked to the crease at number 10.

The hero of the Centenary Test, Rick McCosker, batted through extreme pain and against doctor's orders to rescue Australia.

The advice from the doctors was, obviously, not to bat, and Bob Willis didn't give him a moment's respite, bouncing him first ball. But Rick dug in for an incredible 25 runs, and helped Rodney Marsh reach a terrific milestone with 110 not out. Chappell declared at 9–419, setting England the herculean task of making 463 to win.

After Max grabbed an early wicket, chirpy little Derek Randall from Nottinghamshire, playing his first Test against Australia and promoted in the batting order, took strike. The pair of us proceeded to have an almighty physical and verbal tussle. At one stage Randall fell flat on his back avoiding a short-pitched delivery from me, but, completely unfazed, he merely doffed his cap towards me while prostrate on the ground.

Funny as it is to reflect on his antics now,

they quickly wore thin on me that day, and I told him in no uncertain terms that it takes more than one innings to forge a Test career. Kerry O'Keeffe eventually got rid of him for 174.

The game was on a knife's edge at the tea break when the Queen came out to meet the players. I had arranged for the 12th man, Ray Bright, to slip my autograph book into my blazer pocket, and when Greg Chappell introduced me to Her Majesty I seized the moment and asked for her autograph.

She looked at me, paused and then gestured towards the crowd as if to say, 'If I sign for one person, I'll have to sign for everyone.' Many weeks later, to my great surprise, a letter arrived from Buckingham Palace with a photograph of the moment, signed by HRM! It takes pride of place in my office.

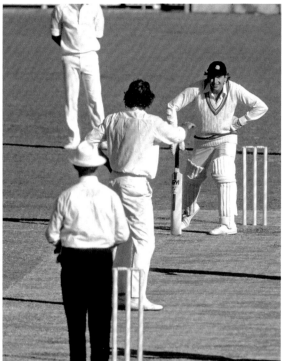

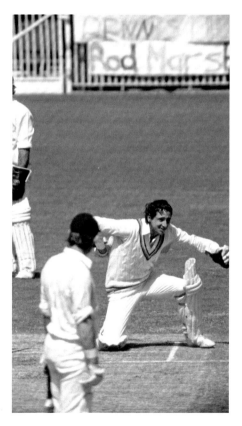

I have grudging and ever-growing respect for Derek Randall's 174 and all-round 'performance' in the 1977 Centenary Test. It was his first Test against Australia and my word, didn't he enjoy it.

*Finally, sweet revenge –
another 'caught Marsh,
bowled Lillee' victim.*

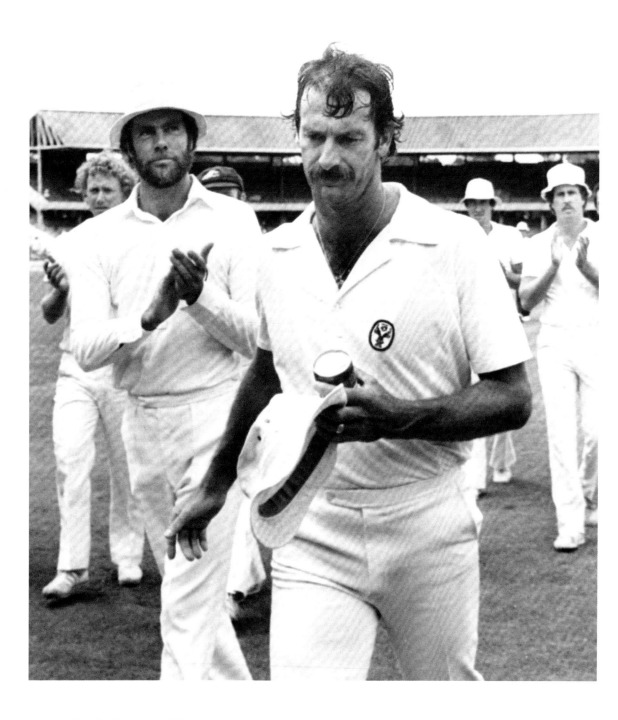

The final session of the Centenary Test was frenetic, England needing 109 with an hour plus 15 eight-ball overs remaining. Tony Greig and Alan Knott were edging England towards their target when the Queen left the ground, and that's when Kerry and I struck. When I trapped Knott LBW for 42, it was all over. Afterwards one wag in the Australian team pointed out that with the Queen still at the ground it would have been disrespectful to wreck England's innings, especially when they were in with a chance of winning.

I had 5–139 from 34.4 overs, and 11 wickets for the match. Australia won by 45

OR
17
LILLEE   5   139
O'KEEFFE   3   108

runs – incredibly, the exact same margin as the first Test match at the same ground 100 years beforehand. But even more extraordinary, I thought, was Rick McCosker's brave effort. His partnership of 54 with Rod Marsh was just about the difference between the sides.

Despite the euphoria, behind the scenes it remained clear that the plans for World Series Cricket were still on the table. There was no turning back now. ●

ABOVE: Being chaired off the MCG by my teammates at the conclusion of the Centenary Test. The crowd was enjoying our win. Nowadays, of course, they wouldn't be allowed onto the ground.

OPPOSITE: It was always nice to get a hand from your teammates after a good bowling performance. I was spent, and looked it.

*What a game! What a finish! The results of the
Centenary Test were exactly the same as the first
Ashes Test 100 years earlier.*

HOWZAT!

I bat for the
WORLD SERIES

© WORLD SERIES CRICKT

PRINTED BY MR TEE-SHIRTS
UNDER LICENCE TO TABULUM HOLDINGS PTY LTD.

Doing my bit to
promote World Series
Cricket in 1978.

6

WORLD SERIES CRICKET

There was a lot of controversy about World Series Cricket. Looking back, it was really terrific cricket and, I've no doubt, was incredibly good for the game.

THE FIGHT WE HAD TO HAVE

WORLD SERIES CRICKET WAS AN INCREDIBLY topsy-turvy time. It's difficult to imagine now because it was nearly four decades ago and, in the end, it turned out to be incredibly good for Australian cricket. But back then, it felt like civil war. There was enormous animosity not just between the players and officialdom, and the players and the media, but also between the players who were in World Series Cricket and the players who were not.

I was in a precarious position, being at once a facilitator determined to stand up for the rights of players and help bring the game into the modern era, and at the same time eager to preserve the heritage and best traditions of cricket.

There were many testing times, particularly in the first year, when we had to scramble to have any sort of pitch and we played in venues that were virtually empty. The first game, Australia against the World XI, was played at the since-abandoned Waverley Park in Victoria, under floodlights erected by Packer. I doubt there were even 200 people there. Typically, the damage the cranes had done putting in the temporary wickets meant the run-up at both ends felt like running through sand.

Invariably the grounds and the interest improved in the second and final year of WSC. I'd say they were some of the finest years of my cricket career. In 15 Supertests, I took 79 wickets at an average of 23.97, which was about my average for all Test cricket. But I consider the wickets I took in WSC even harder to come by than in Test cricket, as the standard was consistently higher.

> It was the toughest cricket I've played; just think about bowling to an opening partnership comprising Barry Richards and Gordon Greenidge! (I still have nightmares about taking them on in the second game at Gloucester Park, a trotting ground opposite the WACA.)

If you lost form there was no way of regaining it against lesser lights as you could in traditional cricket, like Sheffield Shield or club cricket, because you were facing the best cricketers in the world every game. Viv Richards, for example, scored 862 runs at 86.2 in six Supertests. Imagine if those statistics were added to his record. If my wickets had counted, it would have taken me to 434 wickets from 85 Test matches,

The cricket-loving public needed a lot of encouragement to get on board for World Series Cricket, and eventually they did.

Ron Barassi, AFL legend, gives World Series Cricket's Australian players a motivational talk (I'm in the back row, fifth from the left). If my body language suggests I wasn't impressed, it was not because I wasn't impressed with Ron Barassi, but that I felt that motivation can only really come from within.

and there would have been 20 more 'caught Marsh, bowled Lillee' stats.

But I'm just glad it all worked out in the end. I regret the fractured relationships and the turmoil of the time, but I believe the benefits – how it brought cricket into the modern era, and how it was good for players and fans alike – far outweighed the setbacks. One of the key things Packer did was listen to the players, and I believe that is probably the greatest legacy of World Series Cricket. Before then, players were servants to the establishment and had to try to hold down regular jobs on top of playing international cricket. I think there has been a much more equitable balance between players and the establishment ever since, and I hope that always continues. ⬤

About to unleash during the Supertest between Australia and the West Indies in January 1979 in Sydney.

Game changer

Dennis Keith Lillee had the idea for World Series Cricket, and the credibility to convince his fellow players to take a giant leap into the unknown. It would never have happened at that time, and with those people involved, if it hadn't been for him. My friendship with Dennis began when I was playing for Subiaco in the West Australian Football League. Although Dennis was a mad East Perth fan and used to abuse me at games, we got along well.

I was also a cricket writer for Perth's then afternoon paper, the *Daily News*, and used to accompany Western Australia's Sheffield Shield team on tours.

On one tour, in 1972, I suggested to Dennis that I become his manager. The first deal I negotiated for him was an interview with the ABC. I haggled hard and eventually got the ABC bloke up to $200. Unbeknown to me, Dennis had already negotiated $200 for the interview by himself. So, after my commission, Dennis was actually out of pocket on that first job – an inauspicious start to my managerial career, to say the least.

Dennis's major bugbear was the rate of payment to players. He worked so hard to be the cricketer that he was, but then, like all other players, he was expected to hold down a regular job and still be available to meet the increasing demands of the cricket season, including training, Shield cricket, Test series and tours. It was just getting impossible.

Ian Chappell had tried very hard with the Australian Cricket Board to get a decent rate of pay for players, but Don Bradman was the power behind cricket

The SCG lit up for the World Series Supertest Grand Final between Australia and a World XI in 1979.

Twenty-three Australian players. One team played Supertests and the others played against the West Indies or World side in rural venues all over Australia. It was a great opportunity for country fans to see their heroes in their home town.

administration at the time and his word was law. He believed that the pride of playing for your country should be enough incentive (never mind that he had done very well out of cricket himself!).

After 'Chappelli's' experience, Dennis believed that going to the ACB like Oliver Twist with an empty bowl was never going to get the players a fair deal. He thought the cricket authorities had the game by the throat, and the players were like serfs. What they got for playing was really fish'n'chips money – that's how bad it was.

Dennis had become pretty much unemployable because of his cricket commitments. As I recall, he used to earn about $7,500 for playing 12 months of cricket, which included an overseas tour.

After the day's play in Brisbane, Melbourne, or Adelaide, Dennis and I would sometimes end up in the hotel bar talking about life and cricket. More often than not there was one thing on his mind: a better deal for players, and how to get it. Dennis told me that as far as he was concerned the boards and administrators didn't own the game – the players and the fans did. What was needed was a way to bring them together, live and on commercial television (where the money was) so that cricketers could benefit directly from their talent and hard work, rather than have an arbitrary pittance doled out to them by the powers that be. He wanted to see a league of their own, an international competition that brought the best players in the world together on their own terms, and he believed the public would support it.

You've got to remember how audacious Dennis's vision was forty years ago. It was brave, aggressive, on a good length and aimed straight at middle stump. Dennis Lillee thought about cricket the way he played it. It was an unforgettable idea, backed by irresistible logic.

When my footy career ended I moved to Sydney. I was living with John Cornell and his partner, Delvene Delaney. 'Strop' was a part of a new company called CMJ – C for Clyde Packer, Kerry's older brother, M for Mike Willesee and J for John Cornell – producing a program called *A Current Affair* (which John named) and *The Paul Hogan Show*, among other things.

John, Paul and I also started a company called JP Sport, which initially signed all the cricket players and ended up becoming World Series Cricket. When John met Kerry Packer, we were excited because we all knew he was cricket mad and keen to get cricket on Channel Nine. It may have all been far-fetched, but having Dennis on board made the whole thing seem more viable.

> John suggested we play a series of one-day games, but Kerry said, 'Fuck that! We'll sign up all the best players in the world and have our own Test matches.'

This was in January 1977, just eight weeks before the Centenary Test in Melbourne (which, of course, Dennis dominated with an 11-wicket haul). From that moment, the ball just started rolling.

Dennis advised us on who to talk to and when. His support made it so much easier to get all the players alongside. We met with Ian Chappell in Sydney that month. He was the first player we signed.

Then Kerry and Ian pretty much selected the Australian team.

When the Aussies toured New Zealand in February, John and I flew over, met with Greg Chappell and signed him to a five-year contract. The afternoon we left, we signed Doug Walters as well. We had asked Dennis to arrange the meeting in a quiet place, and he got the curator of the ground to let us use some abandoned room, which had nothing but a bare lightbulb hanging from the ceiling. Dougie came in and we were just standing there, looking very dodgy. Doug must have been wondering what the hell was going on. John said, 'Doug, we're a bit short of cash and were wondering if you could lend us fifty bucks?'

Doug, eager to please, said, 'Yeah, yeah,' took out his wallet, and we just fell about laughing.

One by one, we signed up all the Australian players that Kerry wanted (on his say-so, there were four Test players we didn't approach). The Aussies were on tiered contracts, which, in hindsight, was probably a bit of a mistake. We should have given them all standard three-year contracts, which were worth $25,000 a year with a third on signature. Most of the internationals were on this deal.

Tony Greig, who would become so prominent in World Series Cricket, found out about it under funny circumstances. We hadn't approached any of the overseas players when, independently and out of the blue, he requested a meeting with Kerry Packer. Kerry was going around asking how the hell Tony Greig had found out, and we worried there'd been a leak. But it turned out Tony only wanted to ask about potential employment in Packer's organisation down the track.

At that meeting, he was told about the advanced plans for World Series Cricket. He was totally dumbfounded! Tony just could not believe that we had already signed up most of the Australians, especially Greg Chappell, who had seen him just nights before and hadn't let on – Greg has a better poker face than Bart Maverick. Tony wasn't convinced that Greg was on board until I physically showed him the contract.

Ahead of a big meeting with all the players, we realised that we had signed up all of the Australians we wanted – bar one. Although he was instrumental in the whole set-up, we had neglected to contract the main man. I was on the phone to him a couple of times a week, giving him updates on where we were at, and not once did he even prompt us. So Dennis Lillee was actually the last Australian player who got to cuddle his own baby!

Amazingly, despite all this activity, there wasn't a single leak from Australian players. News of World Series Cricket only got out after a big party attended by a few journalists at Tony Greig's house in Sussex during the 1977 Ashes tour in the English summer. The first press about the coming storm was just a single column piece on page one, but almost overnight it became an avalanche of front pages around the cricket world.

Dennis didn't go on that tour of England because he was having some back issues, so we kept him on ice. That upset skipper Greg Chappell because it would critically reduce the team's chances of success in the Test. Kerry wasn't too pleased either, as he had purchased the rights to the Ashes series. But when we explained that it would keep Dennis fresh for World Series Cricket,

Kerry settled back into that glum, relaxed expression he had.

I was sitting in Kerry's office when he rang Bob Parish, Chairman of the Australian Cricket Board, and said, 'We've got some things to talk about.' The conversation lasted less than a minute before Parish just hung up on him. Then it all got pretty hairy pretty bloody quick.

Fortunately, the players were solid, and we had very few waverers. Alvin Kallicharran, the West Indies batsman, got the wobbles and didn't play WSC. He was with Warwickshire, a very establishment county. Dennis and I were with Kerry when he took this call from Alvin, who was copping more pressure than he could handle.

David Hookes got the wobbles too, and he went to Kerry with a lawyer, trying to get out of his contract. Kerry asked him what his problem was, and David said three years wasn't enough. So Kerry gave him a five-year contract, but left Hooksey in no doubt that he'd be chased through the courts should he breach it – and it was a very tough contract.

But it wasn't all serious drama in Kerry's office. One time I was there with Kerry, Tony Greig, and John Cornell and we were all smoking. Kerry said smoking was pure habit: 'I have a theory that you just need something in your hand.' He sent his secretary up the road to buy pipes for us all, and we all sat there sucking on empty pipes with Kerry saying, 'There you go, see?' And then after about 20 minutes of this, Kerry said, 'This is fucking bullshit. Let's have a cigarette.'

When enough players were in place, we were faced with the actual task of putting on the matches. After chasing the signa-

I got along very well with Kerry Packer, and there was no doubting his passion for the game and his belief in the players. Here he is fending off a pretty hostile media in 1977.

tures, I was mostly responsible for player management. But maybe the biggest thing I did was getting the genius curator John Maley on board. Without him we'd still have had contracts and teams, the sneers of the establishment and the excitement of lovers of the game. Trouble is, there just wouldn't have been any cricket! I hope one day I get the opportunity to tell in detail the splendid job that Maley did. He was just magnificent.

It was the Australians who drove the cricketing nations into the court action that followed in England. I was sitting there for six weeks, waiting to see if I'd be called as a witness if it were alleged that the contracts were signed under duress.

Dennis was always there in spirit, through everything. We spent hours on the phone updating and collaborating. Richie Benaud was also there, along with

his wife, Daphne, advising us every step of the way. It was a hell of a time and a hell of a team!

It's important to remember that we never, ever set out to undermine or damage traditional cricket. World Series Cricket was designed entirely to benefit the players and the fans – and, of course, to bring cricket to Channel Nine. But cricket just needed a massive jolt, and World Series Cricket provided it.

I've heard that Kerry Packer dropped around $26 million on World Series Cricket (although cricket on the Nine Network later made him many hundreds of millions). And, four decades on, the game is still on Nine.

While DKL was always a strong right arm, Richie Benaud was our sanity. Rich was always a champion of the players and one of the most revered and respected names in cricket. His hand was never far from the tiller. Richie was very savvy, a master of the game within the game. For example, he strongly advised that our Test matches should not clash with the Board's existing Tests. He was always about what WSC should be doing in the interests of the game, and how to do it. Daphne too. Kerry was seen as a bully – and he sort of was – but Richie softened it all. He and Kerry got along well.

Having Dennis in from the start made it easier to get the players, although to be honest, it wasn't difficult. As Kerry said at the time, cricket was the easiest sport to take over because the players were so badly paid and treated by the authorities worldwide. World Series Cricket on the Nine Network certainly changed things, and for the better. It revolutionised the game for players and spectators, from players' contracts to the technology in television coverage. (Before then, on the ABC, cricket was only televised from one end!) It brought in colours, night games, so much that was new and exciting.

The whole upheaval in world cricket was about the players getting a better all-round deal and then about money. (As it turned out, after working 14-hour days for two years, all I ended up getting was ten grand for my share in World Series Cricket anyway. But that's another story for another time, and nothing to do with Dennis.) Dennis's motivation was about providing a better deal and security for cricketers, as well as giving them a say in modernising a game that had barely changed in one hundred years.

I'm proud of being part of something that did ultimately progress cricket and helped it to remain the national summer game today. It was without doubt the pinnacle of my business career, and up there with my three beautiful daughters Nicola, Danielle and Jacqueline, and induction into the Australian Football Hall of Fame, as the thrilling highlights of my life.

And it all started with a man who had the vision, and the strength of character, to see it through when times got tough. If I were ever in the trenches, I would want to be next to my mate, Dennis Keith Lillee!

Austin Robertson, Australian Football Hall of Fame inductee and central figure in World Series Cricket

Promotional photo for the one-day game. This packaging of the game became the norm during and after World Series Cricket.

Looking wild and woolly in the UK, 1974, a far cry from today.

BARRY RICHARDS

Not deaf, DK!

Fast bowler extraordinaire! Want 110 per cent all the time? Call DKL! My encounters with him go back to 1970. He got selected as a rookie for Western Australia against South Australia, where I had an early victory: BAR 1, DKL 0.

Through the years we had some battles – maybe not as many as we would have liked, due to South Africa's 21 years of isolation from international cricket, but enough for him to occasionally exact revenge.

By the way, Dennis, I did have parents, and was not a $@#%* as you often called me – and not from a distance of 22 yards. I often felt DK thought most batsmen were deaf, as when he said something to us he was awfully close.

World Series Cricket was a godsend for South African players on the outer. The two years where DKL was the frontman of the Australia attack produced some great cricket; his battles with Viv Richards were legendary. Fifty thousand-plus people shouting, 'Kill, kill, kill!' is not inspiring if you have

to open the batting. No wonder helmets came in vogue.

World Series Cricket had its ups and downs, but it was successful because the major players with the most to lose – Lillee, Marsh and the Chappells, plus an up-and-coming David Hookes – made a huge commitment to Packer. Night cricket, white ball, coloured gear plus marketing of cricket as never before was the legacy, and DKL can be proud of that.

I have one little story about Dennis from when night cricket was mooted by John Cornell ('Strop') in the upcoming second year of Packer cricket. At a meeting, JC (no pun!) suggested playing at night, turned to DK and asked his opinion. Rubbing his chin Dennis, in his forthright manner, said, 'No way, too bloody dark!' Vintage Dennis Lillee. And that's why we all love him. I salute you, Mr Lillee!

Barry Richards, 4 Tests for South Africa (during the apartheid era) and 339 first-class matches

SIR RICHARD HADLEE

Trash talk

PBL Marketing Ltd took over the promo- tion of the game on behalf of the Australian Cricket Board and did a marvellous job. Kerry Packer's television techniques, written publications and assorted types of advertising material certainly made people aware that cricket was being played in Australia. During the 1980–81 season, when New Zealand toured Australia, there were posters on hundreds of rubbish bins around the Sydney city area reminding everyone that:

1. 'Lillee bowls at 143 kph.'

2. 'Gavaskar could hook a ball into this bin.' Then a typical Aussie postscript underneath would say, 'Says who?'

3. 'Hadlee can bowl faster than Lillee.' The postscript in bold type underneath read, 'RUBBISH.'

Sir Richard Hadlee, 86 Tests for New Zealand

ONTO MY CLOUD

ANYONE LUCKY ENOUGH TO BE BORN IN THE 'baby boomer' era was able to enjoy, as a teenager, a smorgasbord of high quality rock'n'roll. The so-called British Invasion featured a barrage of talent including, of course, the Rolling Stones with the indefatigable Mick Jagger. Little did I know in those heady days, as I listened to Mick and his band on record, that I would one day become friends with 'rubber lips' himself.

I was introduced to Mick Jagger through a mutual friend while on Australia's 1972 tour of England. During the final Test of that tour, Mick's father, Joe, a member of the Surrey Cricket Club, arranged to meet his son at The Oval to catch up for a pint or two. Mick recalled later that his first look at Test cricket that day reminded him of ballet, as the fast bowlers running in and bowling looked so graceful in his eyes. It just happened to be me who was bowling at the time (and surely the only time my action was described as balletic!)

Fast forward to the 1979 World Series Cricket Supertest in Barbados, where Mick was recording '(You Gotta Walk) Don't Look Back' with Peter Tosh. I noticed Mick sitting in the members stand above our dressing room, and I asked Australia skipper Ian Chappell if I could invite Mick into the dressing room after play. Mick duly came in,

and although shy about being in the dressing room, chatted amiably with the players.

Over the years, as Mick became hooked on the game, we caught up quite often. On one memorable night, when he was recording an album in the Caribbean, he signed the menu for me at the Sam Lord's Castle restaurant in Barbados. He also sent me most of his early albums, signed and with the occasional comment.

On several occasions I was invited backstage to soak up the atmosphere with the Stones, sometimes along with my Australia teammates. In those early days those visits were riotous occasions with raucous music and plenty of booze (not unlike an Australian dressing room after winning the Ashes). On the Rolling Stones' last visit to Perth, I was backstage with Mick and drummer Charlie Watts, also a huge cricket fan, and I was surprised at how the mood had changed – candles, calming music, meditation and no booze (not unlike an Australian dressing room before an Ashes Test). I thought it was a fitting measure of how we all seem to mellow as time (and tears) go by. ●

Mick Jagger's first taste of Test cricket at The Oval, London, 1972.

One of my favourite photographs ever, with me fielding in front of Bay 13 at the MCG. They were as good a crowd as you would find anywhere in the world – especially if they were in your corner. I had a very special relationship with cricket fans, one I've never undervalued.

AUS*** **A
WEST** ***S

7

TESTING TIMES

I had many run-ins with cricket authorities during my
career, but through it all the fans always had my back.
Sometimes it felt like they gave me an extra gear just
when I needed it most.

ORDER RESTORED

Batting against the West Indies in Adelaide, 1980.

I HAD ABSOLUTELY NO FEELING OF GUILT, NOR was I interested in gloating, when I walked onto the Gabba with a unified Test team after the relationship between the Australian Cricket Board and those who took part in World Series Cricket had been repaired. It was 1 December 1979, and the two warring factions had finally reached an agreement whereby Test cricket, as we knew it, was back on the rails.

With Australia captain Greg Chappell having won the toss and electing to bat against the West Indies, there was a warm feeling of wellbeing and business as usual.

The entire West Indies team on that day had played World Series Cricket, and we welcomed Allan Border, Kim Hughes and Rodney Hogg, great players we knew well, back into the best team Australia could field. There was a palpable sense of relief from the crowd. We all felt the same way.

About to deliver the ball in the UK in 1980.

During the WSC period, we were deeply interested in how Australia's depleted official Test team was faring and always had the radio or television in the dressing room tuned in to the ABC. But had I been a member of the public during the hiatus, I would have felt cheated watching second- or third-tier Australia players line up for official Test cricket.

There were times while playing WSC that I thought things would never get back to normal. I had dark fears that we would all face life bans, and that my Test career would end at 30. But once things were resolved, it was up to the selected team to make sure the change was seamless, and for the players to live up to their end of the deal after finally securing the benefits we'd fought so hard for. The only ghost floating around that day would have been in the rooms of ACB administrators who had been so reluctant to listen to our pleas in the first place.

Towards what was to be the end of the WSC era, Kerry Packer's right-hand man, Lynton Taylor, had flown to the Caribbean to meet with the team playing the West Indies. The WSC Australians had drawn up a list of 15–20 demands that we wanted met if we were to resume official Tests. Kerry Packer, through Lynton, wanted to ensure we were totally happy with the outcome. On the top of that list, of course, were the central issues of match payments and authorities listening to players, but we also included things like an improvement in the quality of hotels we stayed at, including one person per room, and a relaxing of rules around our wives being present.

That first Test in Brisbane against the West Indies finished in a draw, but it was still great to all be back playing together again with baggy greens on our heads. My four wickets in the first innings were highly satisfying.

In that 1979–80 season, both the West Indies and England (without the Ashes up for grabs) toured Australia. While Clive Lloyd and his men won the second Test at the MCG by 10 wickets and the third at the Adelaide Oval by 408 runs, we knew from our WSC battles that we were up against the very best there was.

We still felt that we were playing well. That was proven with wins over England by 138 runs, six wickets and then eight wickets in the Perth, Sydney and Melbourne Tests, respectively. I finished with 35 wickets in the six Tests of that summer, with hauls of 6–60 and 5–78 against the Poms at the MCG.

Moments of great satisfaction were trapping Geoff Boycott LBW for a duck at the WACA and bowling him for seven in Melbourne. A busy schedule lay ahead and, now that we were back in the mainstream of world cricket, we were all keen to prove our worth. ●

OPPOSITE: Team photo of the Melville Cricket Club first grade. We won the WACA Premiership with this team in 1979–80. They had never gone close to achieving it in the history of the club. The team included a few state and Test players: Graeme Wood (Aus), Dennis Baker (WA), myself and Kevin Wright (Aus).

Putting Melville on the map

I first met Dennis when I was called into the Western Australia team for the only warm-up match England had in Australia prior to the famous 1977 Centenary Test match played at the MCG.

We drifted apart over the next two Aussie summers as Dennis played in World Series Cricket and I made my way with WA and Australia, but we came together again in the 1979–80 season for WA and at district cricket level with Melville Cricket Club.

Melville CC was a fledgling club in the WACA competition and their administration decided to change things big time, firstly by appointing Dennis as coach and also by attracting a couple of experienced players from other clubs to provide guidance to their younger players.

They didn't know what they were in for. I'm sure pre-season training at Melville had meant a couple of casual weeks' training before the season, and extra physical work meant one lap of the Tompkins Park Reserve prior to walking into the nets. I think we lost half of the old playing list in the first month after Dennis introduced his new training regime. But the extra work soon paid off and the club won its first ever first grade premiership that year. But that was Dennis: either do it his way or find another club.

Not only was he the best fast bowler in the world, but I would also later see that he brought the same focus and energy to everything he did – whether as teammate, mentor or administrator (we worked together at the WACA), and he always had the best interests of the game at heart.

Graeme Wood, 59 Tests for Australia, former chief executive of the WACA

LEFT: Unhappy about the shape of the ball we had to use against Pakistan at the MCG in 1976, I picked up a stray balloon and suggested it would be a better option than the munted ball!

BOTTOM LEFT: I always carried my bat upside down when I left the ground, feeling a bit unworthy as a batsman, I suppose. Here I am leaving the WACA and being greeted by our boys, Adam and Dean.

BOTTOM RIGHT: Shaking hands with Dennis Lillie, a former leg spinner from Queensland. Poor guy was denied access to a flight once, as the ground staff wouldn't believe he was who he said he was!

Feet up and quenching my thirst;
a well-earned rest after a game.

THE OCCASIONAL CONTROVERSY

OVER THE YEARS I WAS INVOLVED IN MORE than my fair share of controversial incidents, with the Javed Miandad stoush and the aluminium bat-throwing episode in Perth probably sitting on top of my list of so-called misdemeanours.

I firmly believe to this day that had match referees been in operation back then, my CV (and hip pocket) would be a lot healthier. I know I overstepped the mark a few times but boy, did I pay for it – I sometimes felt I was at the mercy of everyone. I would have loved to have had a match referee watching on, because these guys, when introduced to the game, were drawn from a wide cross-section of highly-experienced former players, and they could understand a player's perspective.

There was the time at the Adelaide Oval when I was forced off the field with a knee injury after bowling one of the best spells of my entire career – I had taken three wickets in half a dozen balls to set up a Western Australia victory. With the adrenaline still flowing, I was surprised to encounter total silence as I hobbled up the players' race, and I called out, 'Why don't you clap, you buggers?' One of the gin-and-tonic set in the South Australian Cricket Association members' area reported me, and I copped a suspended fine.

Another day, at an almost empty SCG, I cursed my luck when Ian Brayshaw dropped consecutive catches offered by New South Wales leg spinner Kerry O'Keeffe. It echoed right around the empty stands and earned me another fine. (Had it been during a Test match with 30,000 people in attendance, nobody would have heard anything.)

I make no excuses for the Javed Miandad episode at the WACA, but if there been a match referee I don't think I would have been left carrying the can on my own. Years later I saw a television ad that featured several controversial sporting incidents, including the Miandad thing, and as usual it just showed me giving him a soft kick on the pads and him responding with bat raised. What people never saw was the film taken from side-on, which I managed to obtain from an independent source and present at my hearing. It clearly shows Miandad first giving me a not-too-gentle whack in the kidneys with his bat as I was returning to my mark. That clip saved me from a far heavier suspension than the one I incurred. What I did was wrong and I deserved my penalty, but there were two people involved and only one of us copped the rap.

The coming-together with Javed Miandad during a Test between Australia and Pakistan at the WACA in November 1981. It's not a good look, but you can't see what happened before!

Losing it with Javed

Dennis's attitude changed after his injury. Before that, he was never one to drink. But afterwards, he worked on the theory that any day could be his last and he wasn't going to miss out. What never changed, though, was his iron will. It could get him into trouble sometimes, like when Javed Miandad got under his skin.

Javed was one of the few batsmen from the subcontinent who used to genuinely enjoy facing fast bowlers, and the more aggressive they got the more he had the game to combat them. I remember one time Javed was having a bit of luck, a thick edge that Dennis believed should have been caught. He gave Javed a mouthful. I urged Dennis to pitch the bloody ball up. 'Ignore him,' I said, 'he's just trying to get you to bowl short.' Dennis was fuming, but half his anger was directed at Javed and the other half at me for trying to calm him down.

I had three slips and a gully, and a bowler with steam coming out of his ears. Then he shaped up to bowl off spin. 'What are you doing?' I asked.

'I'm bowling effing off spinners.'

'Hold on,' I said.

'You can't tell me what to bowl,' he yelled.

I said, 'Okay, but you can't bowl off spinners when we've got the field set like this.' So I took a few minutes to reset the field, hoping he'd calm down, and brought Rod over the stumps. Then Dennis came in off three or four paces and bowled Javed the best bouncer he'd had all day, nearly knocking Rod's head off. Rod did well to fend the ball off his face and I caught it at the slip.

'What the effing hell are you doing?' I asked. By that stage, Dennis's eyes were practically rolling into the back of his head. I approached him and continued, 'And by the way, you've nearly killed your fat mate.' At that, Dennis almost smiled and settled down a bit. He went back to his long run, took two or three wickets, broke the back of the Pakistan innings and got the job done.

He was quite amazing, really. He would never give up, and won so many matches on his own. To me, one of the marks of Dennis Lillee is shown by how he behaved on one of his least successful tours. We were in Pakistan, and they'd prepared the flattest possible wickets to thwart him. I think he only got about three wickets for the series but not once did he complain or throw the ball back to me and say, 'You might as well bowl.' And, to be honest, he would have had every right to.

Greg Chappell, former captain of Australia, 87 Tests

Hamming it up with teammate Allan Border after the furore over the aluminium ComBat, 1979.

DEFENDING THE COMBAT

THE ALUMINIUM BAT INCIDENT WAS A STORM IN a teacup, but did it ever whip up a frenzy! The prototype of the bat came about at a time when I was in partnership in a Perth indoor cricket centre. The idea was that an aluminium bat would last longer than traditional willow and thus cut costs for cricket institutions over time. It was mainly aimed at practice, as well as country, league and school competition, and not necessarily for grade or first-class cricket. And so the 'ComBat' was born – without a huge amount of fanfare.

In 1979–80, England and the West Indies both toured Australia at the same time, with three alternating Tests being played between the home side and the visitors. The first Test of the season was against the Windies in Brisbane, and I sought permission from the local Queensland authorities to use my aluminium bat when I went to the crease. They weren't overjoyed at the prospect, but said there was nothing in the rules to say I

couldn't do it. And so I went out with the aluminium bat tucked under my arm. Not one of the Windies players realised that it wasn't an ordinary wooden bat.

When I played my first shot, the bat went, *clang*! Desmond Haynes, fielding at short leg, burst into laughter. 'What was that!?' he asked, falling to the ground in stitches. Soon after I was out LBW to Joel Garner for a duck. It was the only time I batted in that Test, so there was no further ado, and the Australian team headed to Perth to play Mike Brearley's Poms.

Once again I checked with local authorities if I could use the aluminium bat, and once again, while they said they were not happy, they were powerless to stop me.

Things came to a head after I drove Ian Botham for three. My captain, Greg Chappell, reckoned that with a wooden bat the ball would have reached the boundary and so he sent 12th man Rodney Hogg out with a conventional bat for me to use. At the same time, Brearley complained to the umpires that the aluminium bat was damaging the ball. I refused to take the willow bat from Hoggy and stormed into the Australian dressing room where I encountered Rod Marsh. He reminded me that I'd been given permission to use the hybrid bat and advised me to go back out and keep using it. Chappell followed me back out and this time insisted that I resume my innings with a normal bat. That's when I snapped and tossed the aluminium one as far as I could.

I escaped a penalty because I had broken no laws, but I was severely reprimanded.

Those laws are now in place, with aluminium bats well and truly banned. My greatest crime was holding a Test match up for 11 minutes.

After that Test, both teams autographed the bat, and Brearley, no doubt with tongue in cheek, wrote, 'Good luck with the sales.' I'd long thought that the ComBat from that day was tucked away in storage or loaned to a museum and could help fund my pension if things got sticky. It was only after getting a contribution for this book from Mike Brearley that I remembered I had gifted the bat to his son. ●

RODNEY HOGG

Rock and a hard place

I was a pretty ordinary 12th man and usu-ally needed encouragement to hurry up, so Greg Chappell had already given me a spray when he sent me out to replace Dennis's bat that day. I felt pretty lonely walking out into the wind at the WACA, knowing that Dennis wasn't expecting me and might not be all that enthusiastic. He was having an argument with Mike Brearley and the umpire, and I'm thinking, *How am I going to get his attention here?*

'Excuse me, Dennis?' I said a couple of times, sheepishly. Now, Dennis couldn't bat, but he looked as ferocious with the bat as he did with the ball, and the mouth guard added something to his snarl. He eventually turned around and barked, 'What do you want?'

'Er, Greg has asked me to bring out these wooden bats to you.'

'Piss off, Hoggy,' he said, 'and tell your captain to go and get stuffed.' With that he turned and walked away. I was out in the middle of the WACA for what felt like a long time, being ignored by Dennis and looking back towards Greg who was calling out, 'Don't you come back here …!'

It's funny because even the way he spat the dummy was so Dennis Lillee. The way he flicked the sweat away, so Dennis Lillee. The headband, so Dennis Lillee. The piercing stare, so Dennis Lillee. The way he appealed, so Dennis Lillee. That voice was so commanding – it was equal parts persuasive (if you were an umpire), intimidating (if you were a batsman) and encouraging (if you were a teammate and Dennis was fielding at mid-off – where you wouldn't normally expect to get much help).

I reckon Dennis has the greatest presence of any Australian sportsperson. He just *owned* the ground. People used to chant his name. Nobody else got that. He *still* gets that. I get 'Rodney who?' while even in his 60s Dennis can incite that chant: 'Lill-ee Lill-ee Lill-ee.' Just amazing.

Rodney Hogg, 38 Tests for Australia

Technically in the right, but in the wrong all the same. This still remains a world record for the longest throw of an aluminium bat in a Test match. A record not likely to be broken.

Mike Brearley, captain of England, and me arguing about whether I could use the aluminium bat. He complained that it damaged the ball. I knew through our testing that it didn't, so we were at a bit of an impasse.

A master in the middle

I've very much enjoyed meeting Dennis on several occasions in recent years. It may be that the longer the gap between the time he was trying to knock my head off (in fact, I think he knew he didn't have to waste too much energy doing that, as he probably only had to bowl a straight ball or two to get me out) and now, the warmer I feel towards him.

Of course, this has only a grain of truth in it. That grain was, for me, that I wasn't too keen on dressing room visits after play

when I knew that the next morning Dennis would be steaming in, the crowd shouting 'Kill, kill, kill,' in a rousing crescendo and accelerando in time with the rhythm of his feet hitting the ground.

We heard rumours that behind the fearsome front was an ordinary good bloke, whom the rest of the Australian team both treasured and took the piss out of. He was said to have made an instantaneous transition from WOT (World's Oldest Teenager) to FOT (Fucking Old Tart).

On stage, in the middle of his arena, Dennis was a master. With his flair for theatricals he was completely at home there. Remember the time when, as an advertising stunt, he came in to bat at Perth in the 1979 Test against England with a metal bat? When, after I had the temerity to complain, the umpires ordered him to change his bat for a wooden one? Captain Greg Chappell marched out in his blazer with a few bats for him to select from; Dennis walked grumpily towards him, looking like a rebellious larrikin, and eventually, with the action of an Olympic discus thrower, hurled the metal abomination away towards the boundary. Geoffrey Boycott, who opened the batting not long after, was soon out (LBW Lillee, 0), we lost four wickets for 41, three of them to Dennis, and Boycott told me I was mad to complain about his tin bat.

But ten years later, when a Veterans match was played between many of the same players, Dennis had gone to the trouble of getting the bat signed by most of those who played in the Test and gave it to my 12-year-old son, who, of course, has it still.

In that same match at Perth, when I stayed in for a while and blocked a few balls back down the pitch to Dennis, he would pretend to be stung by the force of my shot as he picked up the ball. Dennis Lillee was, I reckon, the greatest fast bowler I faced. And there were some terrific bowlers around at that time – Michael Holding and Andy Roberts, Bob Willis and Ian Botham, Jeff Thomson and Rodney Hogg, not to mention Mike Procter and Imran Khan, Richard Hadlee and Malcolm Marshall, and about 20 other West Indians. And on top of this, Dennis was a big figure on the field. He was the person spectators (and the opposition) would keep their eye on. All this was part of his whole package, part of his huge value to his side.

In 2010, when I was in Perth for a meeting and saw a few days of the Perth Test (the only one Australia won in that series, largely due to Dennis's coaching of a previously out-of-form and out-of-confidence Mitchell Johnson), Vic Marks, Tim Rice and I had dinner with Dennis, along with Rod Marsh and John Inverarity (two others, by the way, who are among my favourite Australians). That was when Dennis said, 'We should have spent more time together all those years ago.' He was right. But better late than never.

Mike Brearley, former captain of England, 39 Tests

CENTENARY TEST AT LORD'S

IT'S QUITE SYMBOLIC THAT BETWEEN THE Centenary Tests in Melbourne and London in 1977 and 1980, World Series Cricket rocked the establishment to its very core. These commemorative Tests were celebrating a century of tradition, while the Packer enterprise could only come about because official cricket had held so rigidly to that tradition, and so little had changed in 100 years.

The lead-up to the 1980 Centenary Test at Lord's was just as special as it had been in Melbourne, but this time the match didn't live up to the occasion. As per usual, we were introduced to the Queen, and although I didn't ask for her autograph this time, judging by the chuckles coming from Rodney Hogg I must have said something humorous. Rain ensured that the Test was on, off, on, off and very frustrating for everyone, although I did manage to take Graham Gooch's wicket twice and clean-bowl David Gower.

I was tremendously proud to be only one of four players that day to have also taken part in the Melbourne Centenary Test, the others being Greg Chappell, Rod Marsh and Chris Old. But, as an indication of how things were going during this time, I mostly felt relieved to have got through the occasion without incident. ●

SIR RICHARD HADLEE

Believing in miracles

Just prior to the Centenary Test in 1980, Nottinghamshire had the pleasure of beating Australia by an innings at Trent Bridge.

On each of the three days, there was a 'Player of the Day Award'. On the second day, I won the award by scoring 60-odd and taking two quick wickets. I was presented with a racing bike at the end of the day. I thanked the sponsors and said that I had a problem in getting it home, some 12,000 miles over water. Dennis Lillee, who was standing next to the Notts captain, Clive Rice, turned to him and said, 'With the frigging luck he had today, he could walk on water. I don't know why he can't ride the frigging thing home!'

Sir Richard Hadlee, 86 Tests for New Zealand

The official photo of the Centenary Test at Lord's.

Centenary Test at Lord's in 1980. I'm about to deliver the ball, watched by umpire Dickie Bird, with Mike Gatting at the non-striker's end. In my opinion, Dickie Bird was the best umpire in my playing era.

UNDERARM AND
UNDER PRESSURE

WAS TREVOR CHAPPELL'S UNDERARM delivery underhand? That notorious final ball on 1 February 1981 has become part of cricketing folklore, with its despatch down the MCG wicket dividing two nations.

What I didn't appreciate, and Greg Chappell almost certainly did (coming from a Rugby Union state), was that Brian McKechnie, a 'double All Black', had already established a reputation for lifting his country when all seemed lost.

In 1978 at Cardiff Arms Park, with the All Blacks trailing Wales in the dying seconds, McKechnie had found himself having to kick a penalty goal for victory. He converted what teammate and future All Blacks captain Graham Mourie described as, 'one of the greatest pressure kicks ever taken in Rugby Union'.

Two entirely different thoughts went through my mind when McKechnie threw his bat away in disgust after Chappell's underarm delivery: relief that I could finally rest after an exhausting season, and, deep down, the realisation that this was not in the spirit of the game and would cause a furore.

Tension was high in the dressing room. I decided to get Greg to Sydney with the NSW boys to avoid being hounded in Melbourne. But when we boarded the flight, it was obvious the news had preceded us and all the passengers glared. True to form, Doug Walters lightened the moment by saying, so everyone within earshot could hear, 'Well, Greg, I was always led to believe that a game isn't over until the last ball is *bowled*.'

Later, while in the nets at the SCG No. 2, Doug asked someone to roll a ball down the wicket to him underarm to see what he could do with it. He stuck his foot out to stop the ball and, when it popped up in the air, he hit it out of the ground. 'I can't see what all the fuss is about,' he chirped.

I knew how hard it was trying to maintain peak performance and giving my everything for Australia as a part-time cricketer; I can only imagine the extra strain the burden of captaincy brought. That whole underarm debacle was so out of character for Greg, and I think it was a combination of mental fatigue as well as his fierce determination to win.

We tried to shield Greg from the backlash afterwards and, although he didn't read any newspapers around that time, I'm sure the headlines still haunt him to this day. ●

ABOVE: *The scoreboard reveals the ridiculous odds.*

RIGHT: The Daily Mirror *reflects the controversy.*

FROM A FLUTTER TO A STORM

AT 30 I KNEW THAT I DIDN'T HAVE VERY LONG left as a Test cricketer, so I was determined to give it my all. My back was holding up – and just as well, because an arduous tour of Pakistan in early 1980 was only the beginning of a hectic schedule that also involved a second Centenary Test in England, three home Tests against New Zealand and India, followed by a six-Test Ashes tour.

I was still bowling with good pace, and when the wicket dictated, I bowled cutters off a very short run-up to contain (but still probe) batsmen on a dead wicket. I was still highly satisfied with what I could contribute. But, not surprisingly, the tour of Pakistan was extremely hard work with the wickets and local umpires. Pakistan immediately jumped

to the front with a seven-wicket win in Karachi. I failed to take a wicket from a total of 39 overs, although Ray Bright had a field day in the conditions with 7–87 and 3–24.

During this Test I had so many LBW appeals rejected that I turned to the umpire in despair and inquired what I had to do in order to get him to raise his finger. 'You must hit the stumps with the ball', was his staggering reply.

Australia won the toss in Faisalabad, and Greg Chappell and Graham Yallop put on 235 and 172 respectively. But Pakistan's innings went on for so long that Rod Marsh took the gloves off and bowled 10 overs (and later described the venue as 'Faisala-very-bloody-bad'). I went wicketless, and the match fizzled into a hopeless draw.

The Lahore Test was also drawn, but Allan Border made a name for himself by becoming the first batsman to score in excess of 150 twice in a Test – 150 not out and 153.

The 1981 Ashes campaign started disastrously for me when I was diagnosed with double pneumonia; I lost 10 or 12 kilograms and spent most of the tour on antibiotics. I recovered in time to share in Australia's four-wicket win at Trent Bridge, with figures of 3–34 and 5–46.

The Lord's Test was drawn, but England hit back in the '500 to 1 bet Test' at Headingley, extending their series lead to three to one after the Edgbaston and Old Trafford matches. It turned out to be Ian Botham's Ashes, but most of the credit for Headingley should go to Bob Willis, whose bowling was the greatest sustained effort I'd seen from a fast bowler in all the time I'd played cricket.

I wasn't a big punter, but we had been betting on our games ever since Ladbroke's opened their tents at cricket grounds some years earlier. It was a natural and innocent way to pass the time and the 500 to 1 odds were just too ridiculous to go past. I asked Peter, our coach driver, to put a tenner on and to get the money out of my wallet. Rod told him to grab a fiver for him too.

We didn't even think about the bet until we were sitting in the dressing room after the game, despairing about having lost the Test match. When we realised we'd won by losing, we didn't want to know about it. Our 'winnings' paid for a return trip to Australia and a set of golf clubs for Peter, and helped 'fuel' much of the rest of that tour.

I got 39 scalps in that losing series, outshone by my West Australian teammate Terry Alderman, who finished with 42 wickets from his deadly accurate stump-to-stump deliveries. (Terry took 41 wickets on his next Ashes Tour – what a great bowler.)

After taking four wickets in the drawn first Test against England at the WACA later that season, my right knee collapsed and I missed the rest of the series. I cursed my luck as Greg Chappell led Australia to a 2–1 series win and regained the Ashes.

I was fit enough to play in the one-off Test against Sri Lanka in Kandy in 1983 for which, in hindsight, I'm eternally grateful. Australia won by an innings and 38 runs, but what was most special about that match was David Hookes's unbeaten 143.

Following on from David's exciting debut in the MCG Centenary Test, which had featured a one-over barrage of consecutive fours off Tony Greig, this was the only time the flamboyant and sadly missed South Australian reached triple figures in Test cricket. ●

I can't remember why I was leading the team out – possibly it was my birthday, which fell during that Test at Trent Bridge, the first Test of the 1981 tour.

Confident in my appeal, I was pleased to have Mike Gatting LBW in England's first innings at Headingley, July 1981, but he'd have the last laugh a few days later. Chasing 129 to win, Ray Bright and I got within 18 runs of a win when I got out to a great diving catch by Gatting off the bowling of man of the match, Bob Willis. Ray and I put on 35 after Australia were 8–75 but we just couldn't get it over the line.

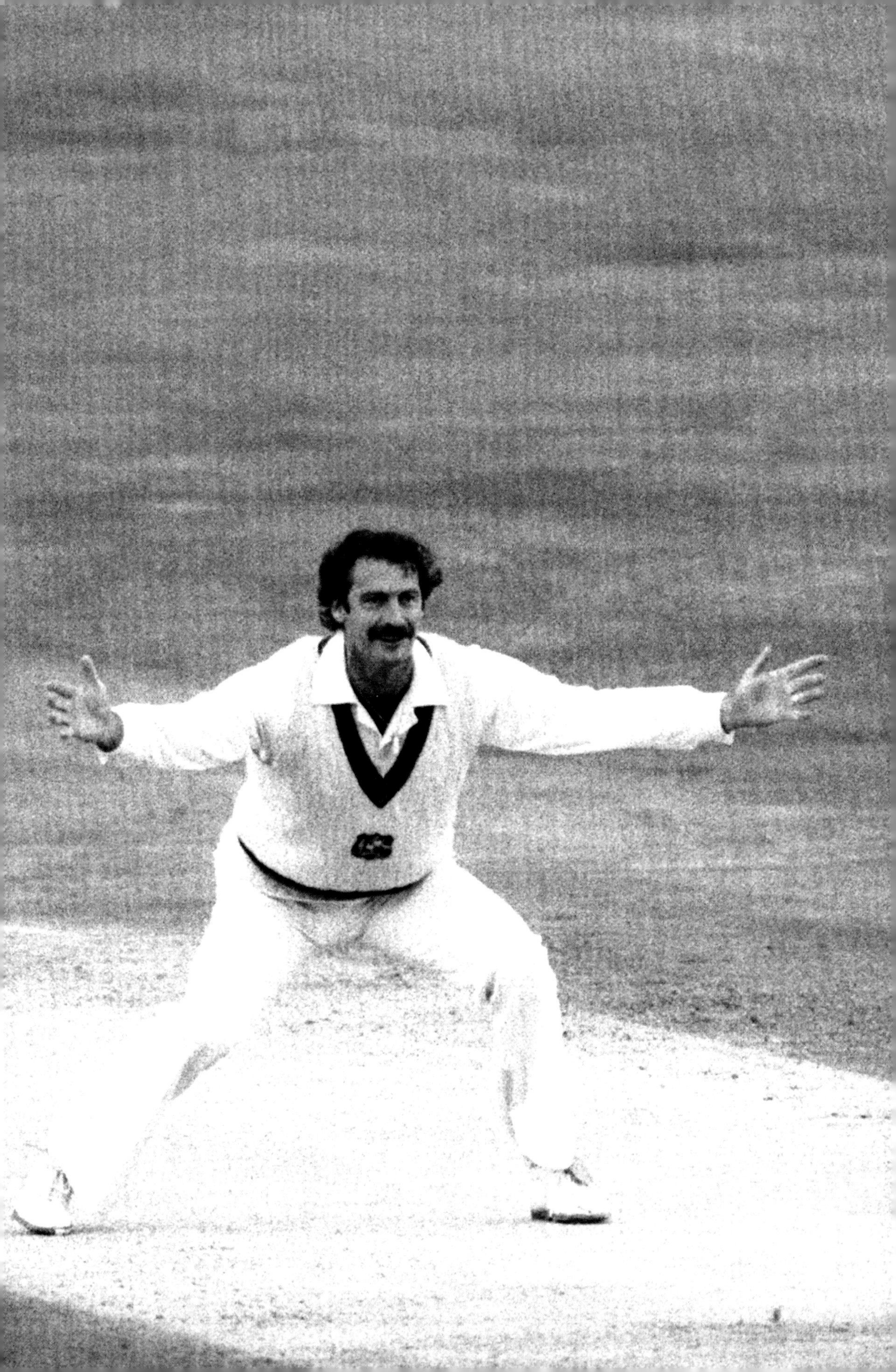

ABOVE: This is a pretty serious signal. Maybe I had just got someone out for a duck and was reminding them. The headband was to advertise my upcoming benefit year in Australia. It didn't last long as I was told to lose it!

RIGHT: Drinks with Allan Border and John Dyson at the White Hart Pub in Worcester. Dick and Nan Thomas had the whole touring party there for lunch. They were great friends to Aussie Cricket teams and ended up migrating to Esperance in WA.

Touring the UK in the early 1980s.

LEFT: I swapped an Aussie baggy green for a bobby's helmet. I bet he would've gotten into trouble if he was found out. He'd be laughing now, though!

BOTTOM LEFT: Dirk Wellham, me, Allan Border, Graham Yallop and Len Pascoe (I think), possibly settling an argument about cricket stats using the Google of the day.

BOTTOM RIGHT: Writing letters home or answering letters of support. Finding the right words was always hard – note the scrunched-up failures at my feet.

X factor

My brother and I used to try to be like
Lillee and Thomson in the backyard. I
wanted to be DK but I was never going to
have that pace. I tell kids now, 'You've got
to have your heroes, the players you want
to emulate,' and Dennis was definitely one
of mine.

Next thing I know, I'm 16 and get a
lucky break with the wicket of John Inverarity in a grade game in Perth. 'Inver'
must have gone to the state selectors and
told them he'd been knocked over by a
16-year-old bowling outswingers, and I got
selected for the state team. My mum always told me to address my elders as 'Mr',
so I'm down at the WACA saying, 'Yes, Mr
Inverarity, yes, Mr Marsh, yes, Mr Lillee.'
They fell about laughing until Rod eventually sidled up me and said, 'Mate, just call
me Rod.'

Jump forward to my Test debut and
the 1981 tour of England, and I'm opening
with Dennis Lillee for Australia. We were
practising in the nets when Dennis spotted
something about the length of my run-up
and suggested I be a bit more aggressive
at delivery stride to get better balance.
Whatever it was, something clicked.

Dennis was particularly good at looking
out for teammates like this. And whatever
Dennis said, blokes listened. He was the
guru. He helped me get a better handle
on the Duke ball, the standard ball used
in England, which is bigger in your hand
and has a more pronounced seam (I still
don't think we do enough lead-up practice
with the Duke ball). We needed every little
advantage we could get because, remember, in those days, it was part-timers (I
was a primary school teacher) for Aus-

tralia against full-time professionals. The
sheer weight of numbers was also stacked
against us; we had five Shield sides at the
time, against England with something like
19 or 20 county teams.

While I was in good nick for that tour,
Dennis was anything but. Not only was he
managing his back problem, but he had
to be hospitalised in London after getting a bout of pneumonia. Added to that,
he'd got permission from MCC to train
at Lord's, but when he arrived the gate-
keeper wouldn't let him in! (Every time we
arrived at Lord's in the coach after that,
we used to give that guy heaps.)

There he was, coughing and splutter-
ing, and I didn't think he'd be able to play,
to be honest. But his underlying physical
condition was just incredible, and his work
ethic and fitness carried him through. He
had a program of biomechanic exercises to
support his back, and I was the guinea pig
sent to assist him. I remember having to
hold him at one stage, and just feeling the
power from his back was incredible.

I still can't quite believe we lost that
tour. It was just ridiculous to lose at Headingley. If we'd won that, we would have
been 2–0 up in the series and would never
have lost. I took 42 wickets in that series,
thanks partly to bowling alongside Dennis.
Between us, we took 81 wickets and still
lost. But the fact that Dennis was able to
contribute the way he did, given the state
he was in, was quite remarkable.

He had a sort of laser-like focus that
wouldn't let up. I remember playing Shield
cricket years before – I think Rod 'Bacchus'
Marsh was captaining Western Australia

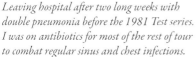

Leaving hospital after two long weeks with double pneumonia before the 1981 Test series. I was on antibiotics for most of the rest of tour to combat regular sinus and chest infections.

What a tragedy for great WA and Australia fast bowler, Terry Alderman. After being hit by a drunk spectator, he chased the man down and tackled him to the ground, injuring his shoulder in the process and threatening his great career.

at the time, and Dennis and Mick Malone were opening. After 40 minutes, Bacchus told me to warm up: 'Clemmie, you're on next.' I was eager to get going but we couldn't get the ball off Dennis and I didn't get to bowl for the entire first session. I think he must have had Greg Chappell in his sights that day or something, but that was typical Dennis. Sometimes the hardest task the captain had, even when playing for Australia, was how to get the ball off Dennis and convince him to take a spell.

But nobody complained, because he was Dennis Lillee and it was fantastic to be part of it. What a weapon to have. It was like in that Test against the West Indies at the MCG, on a flat, hard wicket. He was soaking up the atmosphere, and Bay 13

was going crazy. There was no chance the umpire could even have heard a nick over the chants of 'Lill-ee, Lill-ee.' It was a real hairs on the back of your neck time. And in the last over, there must have been 5000 people already on the ground, but still Dennis kept going until the last ball, cleaning up Viv Richards in a memorable performance.

Nobody else in Australian cricket had that 'X factor', at least not consistently – the ability to work the crowd, the raw ability, the rebellious streak, the physical strength. Add to that his ability to transition from a runaway train with his arms all over the place at the start of his career to the Rolls-Royce of actions. Just incredible.

Terry Alderman, 41 Tests for Australia

Even when we curtailed his batting – we had him 'caught Marsh, bowled Lillee' for three in the second innings – Beefy took to us with the ball. He took five wickets for 11 runs in our second innings. No wonder the 1981 series is known as 'Botham's Ashes'.

STOUSHES AND STATESMEN

YOU DON'T GET TO THE TOP OF WORLD CRICKET without some aggression, but you'd be amazed at the differences between the 'normal' and 'competitive' personalities of top cricketers.

There have been plenty of verbal sprays in the heat of competition but very rarely has anything got out of hand. Examples that spring to mind are Steve Waugh having a blue with Curtly Ambrose, and Glenn McGrath getting fired up with Ramnaresh Sarwan. Off the field, though, Waugh is a total diplomat and McGrath wouldn't say boo to a goose. But compare those verbal aggressions to the tactics used by Douglas Jardine during the bodyline series. Which was more violent?

I can only recall two players ever throwing a punch: once when a frustrated Rodney Hogg had an air swing at his skipper, Kim Hughes, and once when Kepler Wessels worked out with the punching bag in the gymnasium. There has sometimes been a bit of pushing and shoving after hours, and a disagreement or two on an aircraft, but 99.9 per cent of cricketers I've known are gentlemen.

Ian Botham pushed the boundaries a bit because of his nature. I'm not saying he came out swinging, but he wouldn't take a backward

On the rest day (yes, we had rest days!) at Yalumba winery in the Barossa Valley, South Australia, chewing the fat with one of the greatest all-rounders of our era, and of all time: Ian Botham. December 1982.

step if there was some aggression towards him. He simply hated people having a go at him. But you have to understand that he was huge in cricket, especially in England. When you're in such a lofty position there is always someone who wants to have a go at you. Because Botham was so aggressive on the field, some took that as a sign that he was aggressive in his everyday nature. But you only need to look at all the wonderful charity work he's done in England to see the other side of his personality and why he was knighted.

During his playing days, Botham brought a few things on himself, and there have been several versions of his infamous run-in with Ian Chappell. But as hard a nut as Chappell was on the field, he would walk away from a fight rather than be involved in one. Often the way people are perceived on the field has nothing to do with what they are like off it.

These days some leading players are victims of tall poppy syndrome, which can lead to distorted attention and criticism. Back in the pre-television days, on-field exploits were confined to ABC radio and the occasional black-and-white newspaper photograph, and so most incidents flew under the radar.

As far as being pestered while I was out with my teammates, I rarely had a problem or got stuck somewhere I didn't want to be. If the conversation dragged on, I'd say I was with my mates and ease myself away. If that didn't work, we had prearranged 'get me out of here' signals, which worked with military precision. The front guard would approach and just sort of shuffle the captive back into the group.

I think the pressures are much more intense these days, as are the risks, which is why players are often so highly managed. But if cricketers can't do what they've done for the past 140 years and head for the local watering hole with their mates at the end of the day, then it is a sad situation indeed. ●

ABOVE: 'Beefy' Botham telling a story during a stopover in India on our way to England for the Centenary Test. England were playing a Test series against India, and we turned up at the game in Bombay to watch a few hours' play.

LEFT: Another cartoon I was sent and kept.

Bowled and bailed by Lillee

'It's okay, I've got hold of DK, and he's with his lad who can sign too ... Only problem is they're a couple of hours away, so you'll have to sit tight for a little while longer.'

I was relieved. My solicitor, Alan Herd, had only just landed in Perth along with my wife, Kath, to watch me play for Queensland against Western Australia in the 1988 Sheffield Shield final – and I was in jail.

It wasn't really my fault, of course. There'd been an argument on the flight over between Greg Ritchie and Allan Border that I had somehow been dragged into after trying to keep the peace. The language was a bit too rich for a passenger in front. I told him to mind his own business and I turned his shoulders round to face the front. Technically that is an assault, but where I come from it is nothing more than friendly encouragement.

Anyway, I needed bailing out. West Australian law dictates you must be signed out by two landowners from the state, hence my need for a local friend – and who better than DK Lillee to ride to the rescue? He turned up with his son to bail me out, as promised, but he went above and beyond in bringing a six-pack of beer and a bottle of Bundaberg with him. These were all consumed in my joy at being released and my anger at having to prepare for a final in the lock-up. (I realise now that downing this lot probably wasn't the best preparation either!)

Dennis had hung up his boots after a few games for Tasmania in that season, but our relationship on and off the field went back years. We'd had some fantastic Ashes battles. There is no doubt in my mind that DK was the finest pace bowler of his generation. To pass him as the leading Test wicket-taker in the world was a huge honour, but I always had clear in my mind who was the better bowler.

I got to face him many times, usually without much success, but one game in particular stands out. It was again in Perth, where he was king of the castle. We had gone out to play Australia in 1979 once all their World Series Cricketers were back in the fold. I was batting in the second innings after bowling pretty well, taking 11 wickets.

Dennis was standing at the top of his mark, and all I could see in the bright sunshine was the medallion around his neck glinting in my eye as he started to charge in. Rod Marsh was standing miles back, and I played and missed as Dennis followed through towards me. I played and missed again at the next one as Dennis finished a little closer. When I played and missed for a third time, Dennis's follow-through now had him just one yard away from me.

He ran his finger across his sweaty brow and flicked the sweat onto my shirt. With a growl, he said, 'I thought you were supposed to be able to bat?! Just hold the bloody bat still and I'll hit it for you.' There were a few more colourful phrases in there that I can't quite remember. Next ball I got into position early, and would you believe it, the ball hit the middle of the bat. He really was that good.

Sir Ian Botham, 102 Tests for England

And well might he look confident on the way to 118 and an England win at Old Trafford in August 1981.

THE TOUGHEST AUSTRALIANS

I PLAYED WITH A FEW HARD-AS-NAILS CHARACTERS during my time. These guys are top of my tough list.

The baggy green cap meant everything to **Ian Redpath**. He was prepared to end it all out there! Being a bloke with not much meat on him, Redpath copped countless blows to the body, which would have been extremely painful – but he never flinched.

Although my first Test was **Bill Lawry's** last, I was in awe watching and hearing how this guy would come out of an innings black and blue and just keep coming back for more. While playing a Sheffield Shield match against us on a very fast pitch at the WACA, he was hit time and again (including by me), but went on to score a century. A lesser player would have simply chucked in the towel.

Rod Marsh's attitude was 'never give a sucker an even break', even when Rod was playing with fractured fingers. He admitted that it really hurt keeping to Thommo and me because we hit his gloves so hard, but he always said the pain was worthwhile.

There was no quarter taken or given with **Ian Chappell**, who had absolute faith in his players and was prepared to back them all the way – both on and off the field. He could handle anything. There was action for Chappell right from the word go; his first

Test in charge featured the infamous Ray Illingworth-led SCG walk-off.

My opinion of **Bruce Laird's** courage under fire is shared by a pretty illustrious group of blokes. The mighty West Indian pace bowlers said they rated no opening batsman in the world more highly than Laird.

How tough was **Allan Border**? He was given his Australian spurs when the West Indies were still at their peak, and no captain has had a more demanding initiation than the gritty little left-hander. Thrown in at the deep end when Kim Hughes resigned, Border proceeded to lead, gallantly, some far from awesome Australian line-ups. He always led by example and, after

England captain Ray Illingworth talks to the umpire ever so diplomatically after John Snow (left) has been warned about bowling too many bouncers during the 1971 Test at the WACA. Snow and Bill Lawry await the outcome, but I doubt it would have phased Bill Lawry either way.

much perseverance, nobody could begrudge him his success when he led Australia to a comprehensive yet unexpected Ashes series win in England in 1989.

I've admired the toughness of many players whose careers didn't coincide with mine – too many to mention – but Steve Waugh and Justin Langer immediately spring to mind.

Apart from his resolve under difficult situations in the middle, Steve Waugh had the incredible ability, through hard work, to recover from serious injury in time to get back on the field.

And Justin Langer forces his way onto my list through his sheer tenacity and willpower. Langer started his career with a baptism of fire, then almost fell into oblivion before fighting his way back to establish himself as a fine opener and, later on, a successful coach. Hope I haven't forgotten any! ●

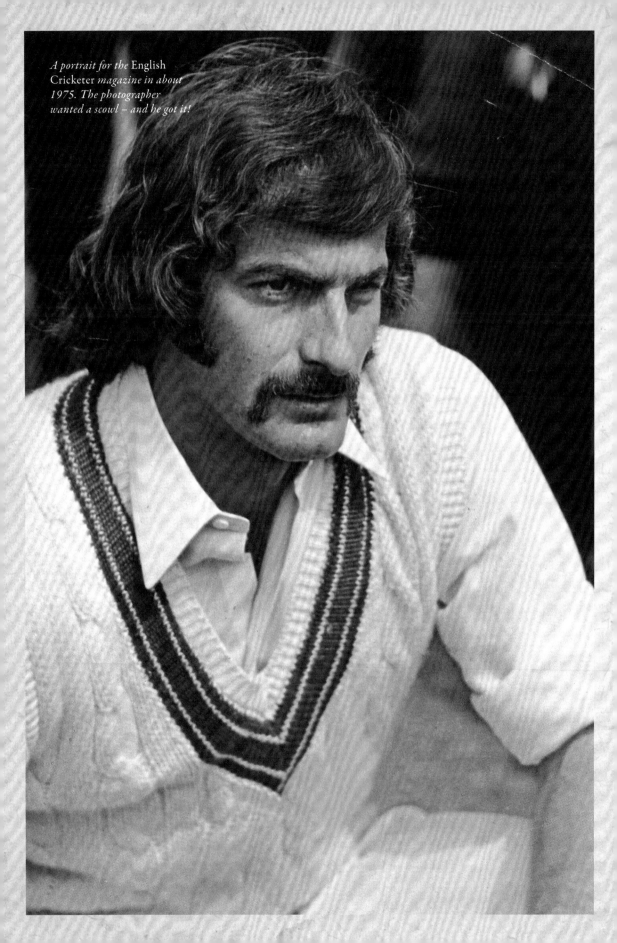

A portrait for the English Cricketer magazine in about 1975. The photographer wanted a scowl – and he got it!

8

BREAKING RECORDS

After my injury I never looked too far ahead in my career. I was happy to be fit and in the team, so records were the last thing on my mind. That's why breaking Richie Benaud's record for the most Australian Test wickets was so unbelievably special.

STUNNED AND RELIEVED

THE 1980–81 SEASON BEGAN WITH A FLURRY OF wickets against New Zealand, and the media got fired up about the prospect of me setting the Australian record for the most Test wickets.

I began with eight wickets in Brisbane and seven in Perth, although I only managed one wicket in the drawn MCG Test. Against India later that summer, the wickets continued to tumble and Richie Benaud's record came within sight. We beat them by an innings in Sydney – Len Pascoe and I got four wickets apiece while they managed only 201. (Greg Chappell outscored them with 204!) India were much more competitive in the drawn Adelaide Test, where I got another six wickets.

And so the stage was set for my assault on Benaud's record in Melbourne. We bowled India out for 237 and put them under pressure with 419 in our first innings. They started their second innings well, with Sunil Gavaskar and Chetan Chauhan sharing an opening stand of 165 before I trapped Gavaskar right in front for 70. I'd equalled Richie Benaud's record for Test wickets – or had I?

We were sure it was clean, and so was the umpire, but Gavaskar just stood there, whacking his bat against the pads in anger, insisting the ball had hit his bat first. In a massive dummy-spit, Gavaskar, the captain, then proceeded to lead his reluctant batting partner off the ground. I'm sure it had something to do with his frustration at having never posted a big score against me.

But sanity prevailed when the team manager met the pair at the gate, first to order Gavaskar into the dressing room and then to ask Dilip Vengsarkar to accompany Chauhan back to the middle.

The incident must have also affected Chauhan, who was on 85, because shortly afterwards he slashed at a delivery I pitched wide of off-stump, and Bruce Yardley took the significant catch.

I simply couldn't believe, after making Indian opener Chetan Chauhan my 249th Test victim, that I'd not only gone past Richie Benaud but had left one of my great heroes, Graham McKenzie (246 Test wickets), behind too.

The record was overshadowed a little by Gavaskar's antics, but I wasn't particularly bothered. I didn't think much about records in my career because to be honest, after my injury, I never thought I'd last the distance. But of tremendous importance and pride to me was that I passed Richie Benaud's milestone when the great man himself was present, commentating on the match. I proudly waved to him high in the stands. It was a gesture I would never even have dreamt of making when I first picked up a cricket ball. The great man personally delivered a bottle of champagne to the dressing room to congratulate me afterwards.

Sunil Gavaskar, given out LBW, argues that he got a bit of bat on ball and shouldn't have been out. I thought that his argument should have been with the umpire who made the decision, not me, of course. I mentioned that to him before explaining which way the dressing room was.

While that first milestone was reached with incredulity, the next, Lance Gibbs's world record for Test wickets, came, eventually, with great relief.

I should have taken the record in the final Test against Pakistan in the 1981–82 series. Channel Nine had even brought Gibbs, the West Indian spinner, out to Australia for the occasion. I needed five wickets but didn't even take one. It was a massive let-down. At the end of the game I thought it was very possible that I would never take another Test wicket. If I lost confidence and didn't take a wicket in the next Test, there was every chance I could be dropped.

The next match was the Boxing Day Test in Melbourne against the West Indies. Batting first, we made only 198 but immediately put them under pressure. Given the opportunity to bowl for the last half hour, Terry Alderman started a West Indies collapse by dismissing Faoud Bacchus for one. I followed by getting rid of Desmond Haynes for the same score, and then Colin Croft, who'd come to the wicket as a nightwatchman, LBW for a duck. Viv Richards then launched a drive, got an inside edge and was bowled for two. The Windies were 4–10 at stumps as the crowd heaved with excitement.

I had three for three in the space of 12 deliveries and was now only one wicket away from drawing level with Gibbs. But I had to wait for a while. The next day, when Clive Lloyd, Larry Gomes and Jeff Dujon began to get hold of us, my confidence in breaking the record began to sag again. My cause wasn't helped when the normally super-reliable Greg Chappell dropped Gomes.

Then halfway through the afternoon session I got wicketkeeper Dujon to hook, and Kim Hughes took a very well-judged running catch that enabled me to draw level with Gibbs. Thirteen runs later, shortly before three o'clock, I got Gomes to wave his bat outside off-stump and Chappell took a catch identical to the one he had previously dropped.

The record was mine. The relief was palpable. I bowed my head, then raised it to savour the moment with my teammates – in particular Rod Marsh, who had shared in 83 of those dismissals. In a haze I wandered off in the wrong direction when I should have been heading towards deep fine leg. Nobody seemed to care, though, and once I got to where I was supposed to be, it all sank in.

Both records were extra special because I was in the right place at the right time. I'm not sure the moment would have been quite the same had I been in some lonely cricketing outpost, such as Faisalabad in Pakistan. That both milestones were achieved in front of the hugely appreciative and genuinely excited MCG crowds was, well, the stuff of boyhood dreams. ●

Polishing the ball and acknowledging Richie Benaud in the MCG press box after breaking his record for the most Test wickets by an Australian.

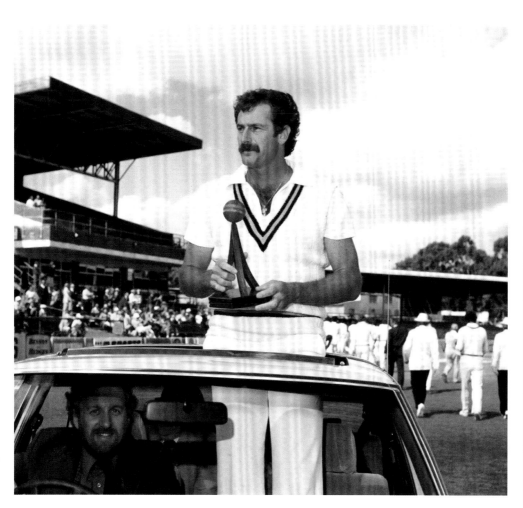

ABOVE: Doing a lap of honour at my beloved home ground, the WACA, after breaking the Australian record for most Test wickets.

Checking the old-style scoreboard in the UK, where they kindly put up '355' to show the total number of Test wickets I'd taken in my career.

HAVING A LEND OF
DICKIE BIRD

T HE WORD THAT MOST ACCURATELY DESCRIBES
Dickie Bird is probably 'eccentric', but he
was the best umpire I have ever come across.
He was hard but fair, and, importantly,
underneath it all he was a totally decent
human being who endeared himself to
cricketers around the globe. The thing that
underpinned the relationship between
Dickie and the players was respect. There was
always give-and-take with him, and players
knew where they stood.

For example, during the final Test at The
Oval in 1975, England scored 538 during a
second innings that lasted 886 minutes – more
than two days' play – and we were having a fair
bit of trouble with the balls being used during
that marathon innings on a very hard pitch.

The ball looked like it had been through a
mincer, and I told Dickie that I simply wasn't
going to bowl with it any more. If batsmen
could change damaged bats, why did I have to
bowl with an impaired ball?

'No. Please continue the over,' said Dickie,
unmoved. I dug my heels in and, after captain
Ian Chappell was dragged into the matter,
Dickie promised to have a look at the ball at
the end of the over. Chappell told me to bowl
the remaining two deliveries. I said I would, but
only by bowling off spinners. Typically, Dickie
defused the situation by telling me they were

two of the best off spinners he had ever seen,
which just made me laugh.

I confess, some of us did try to take
advantage of Dickie from time to time. As
a result of his affability, players, including
myself, felt confident enough to play a few
little tricks on him without fearing massive
reprisals. If you tried to pull the same pranks
with some international umpires of that era
you would have undoubtedly left yourself
open to penalties.

On one occasion, Ian 'Beefy' Botham went
out to bat just after he'd taken a big plunge on
a horse. Anxious to know the result of the race,
he took his mobile phone out to the middle
and handed it to an unsuspecting Dickie.
Predictably, the phone rang, and when Dickie
answered it a voice said, 'Tell Beefy his horse
lost.'

Suddenly Dickie froze, as if he was holding
a hand grenade. He was no doubt terrified
of being perceived as part of a prank by the
fuddy-duddies watching from the official area.
Imagine how the television cameras would
zoom in on an incident like that these days!

England batsman Allan Lamb, a great
prankster, once had a hilarious get-square after
he thought Dickie had incorrectly given him
out. Lamb and some of his mates got four
chocks and raised Dickie's car a few centimetres.

Not only was Dickie Bird a character, he was an absolute gentleman and the best umpire of my era. Here he is protecting the stumps while the crowd invades the pitch to celebrate a West Indies win against England at The Oval in 1976.

At the end of the day, Dickie failed to notice his car was slightly off the ground, and everyone in on the prank nearly split their sides laughing at his futile attempts to leave the carpark.

Dickie was a jittery sort of bloke who, to his detriment, let it be known that he was terrified of snakes. I got hold of a large rubber snake that a teammate had found in a novelty shop in London.

During lunch at a Lord's Test match, I didn't feel like eating because Australia was in the field, so how else to pass the time? I grabbed the attendant just as he was about to deliver lunch to the umpires in their little room at the top of the stairs. I swapped Dickie's lunch with this fake snake and put the metal cover back over his plate.

Well, the commotion that erupted was astonishing. Dickie dropped the plate on the floor and almost knocked the door off its hinges as he burst out of the room and ran down the stairs. I'm glad Dickie never discovered that I was the culprit – it was hard enough getting an LBW decision from him as it was! ●

Impersonating the great man at The Oval in 1981.

*OPPOSITE: At Lord's in 1993, possibly the moment
Dickie realised it was me who replaced his lunch with
a plastic snake.*

Life in your own hands

Once you made runs against Dennis or Thommo, you knew you had been in a battle, and that it would be an innings to remember. You also knew you were taking your life in your hands, because we didn't wear helmets in those days and they were that quick.

I made a couple of hundreds against Dennis, but you could never risk a moment's carelessness or say that you dominated him. He was always working out ways to get your wicket, and I've no doubt he was one of the best fast bowlers I've ever seen.

As a captain, I could appreciate that Dennis was an incredible bowler to have in your team when you were looking for a breakthrough. He won games on his own on quite a few occasions. He was the ultimate workhorse and professional, even when the wicket wasn't conducive to fast bowling.

I picked up a lot from Dennis where training was concerned. After we played against Australia in 1975–76, and lost 5–1, I decided that was the way we should go. In the second Test, when we had a full complement of bowlers, we won in three days so I knew we were on the right track. But I got tired of drinking champagne in the opposition dressing rooms!

Australia had a very strong team in that era, very professional and well-led by the Chappells. They played hard and drank hard, but managed to put those two things together successfully. The great West Indies teams had those same characteristics, and Dennis Lillee would have made it into any team in his day.

We got on so well and we never had bad words. Perhaps that's partly because I'm very placid and never got into sledging or any of that. I remember once when he bowled an inswinger, and I caught the inside edge onto my pad. Then Dennis said, 'We've been down this fucking road before,' but he was never aggressive to me.

Whatever happened on the field, you'd sit down for a drink with him and he'd make you feel like a brother. I always insisted on having a drink with the opposition when I was a player and a manager. They don't do that these days, and I think they're missing out.

To me the best thing about cricket is the lifelong friends that you make. Those relationships are built on passion for playing cricket, fierce competition, the sharing of unique experiences and mutual respect. I treasure those moments.

Dennis epitomises everything that is good about cricket, and showed that you can be a fast bowler and still be a very honest and gentle person. He put fast bowling at the top, really. His action was perfect and it's no wonder he was idolised all over the world. He is a terrific person for our game.

Clive Lloyd AO, former captain of the West Indies, 110 Tests

Two of my fiercest competitors, yet among the most placid and polite people you'll ever meet, West Indies captain Clive Lloyd and England captain David Gower before a Test at Edgbaston in 1984.

A polite rivalry

There are all sorts of words that might describe the experience of facing Dennis Lillee from the other end of a cricket pitch: challenging, exhilarating, daunting, inspiring and many more besides. I'd also use the word 'proud'; I'm proud to have had that experience.

There were few more exhilarating sights in cricket than that of DK Lillee in full flight. I recall watching him on my television set as a teenager in the mid-1970s, steaming in at Lord's with that iconic 70s hair streaming behind him, and England's batsmen shuffling into line to try to cope with his thunderbolts. In those days, Dennis might admit to being a bit wayward, but batsmen will admit that waywardness made their job harder.

My first Ashes tour was in 1978, during the Packer years. Watching Channel 9 for the first time, we, as the 'official' tourists, were rapt watching the 'rebels' strutting their stuff in World Series Cricket. It was awesome cricket to watch, and Dennis was definitely one of its greatest stars, the master not just of his craft but of confrontation and showmanship.

A year later I was back in Oz on what might be described as the unification tour. Packer had won his argument, and Australia, now at full strength with Dennis, Marsh and both Chappells all back in the fold, hosted England and the West Indies in a summer that was intended to bring 'official' cricket back to the fore. Cunningly, England agreed to tour that year only so long as the Ashes were deemed not to be at stake. Three Tests

and three wins (for Australia) later, that was just as well!

I got my first 'caught Marsh, bowled Lillee' in the book at the first attempt in Perth (best to get things out of the way early), but I redeemed myself in the second Test at the SCG. There, I finished in the second innings 98 not out. It was my fault – I exposed my number 11, Bob Willis, to the strike at just the wrong moment. It was also one of 'those' innings – the first 30 or so came either through or over the slips down to third man, and then finally I rediscovered the middle of the bat.

As I recall, Dennis and I never quite had the same issues as he and Derek Randall. (Mind you, no one could genuinely dislike Derek, even in his most Norman Wisdom-like mood!) DK and I used to exchange words, yes, but seldom, if ever, in an antagonistic fashion. I don't suppose DK was used to batsmen apologising if they nicked it over the slip, and there were many knowing glances or shrugs of the shoulders exchanged if I played and missed, or if I despatched him authentically to the boundary.

In the course of it all, and through our subsequent meetings, I'm happy and proud that a certain mutual respect evolved. To be frank, it is the sort of contest that helps you define yourself as a younger player coming up against a legend of the game. In my formative years, playing against that Australian team was the ultimate challenge.

Three years after that 1979–80 tour we were back (with the Ashes now up for grabs again) and there were more knowing looks and quizzical glances. In the state match at the WACA before the first Test, I took on DK's bouncer in the second innings. I hit it pretty well, I thought, and was just watching the result to see if it carried for four or six, only to see it end up in the hands of Greg Shipperd at wide long leg. There was no extravagant send-off – just another knowing look!

DK played the first Test but had to miss the rest of the series. As ever in Ashes cricket, his absence didn't make for an easier contest, but it was definitely the contest-within-the-contest that I missed. I have a feeling that he made it to the rest day in Adelaide. (I might be muddling up years and memories, but I'm quite certain it was that year.) Both sides made it to the Hill-Smith family's wonderful Yalumba Estate to eat their food, drink their wine, mess around in the pool and, most demanding of all, find our way back to Adelaide at the end of the day. No pressure for Dennis as he was not due on the field the following day – though come to think of it, I don't remember any of those who were due to perform feeling the pressure either!

If there was any pressure on him, it came in the inevitable shape of Ian Botham, a man whose sense of mischief and exultation in excessive horseplay was undoubtedly fuelled by the combination of Yalumba wines (in proper quantities), sunshine (in proper quantities) and a swimming pool. There was indeed no peace for the wicked, or even the innocent, while Botham and Lillee dunked each other time after time into the deep end.

Although rest days are now consigned to the bin, and rightly so, they were often bloody good fun. It is bizarre to think that in the middle of one of the ultimate sporting battles – an Ashes Test – both teams could get together in such circumstances, behave as the best of friends and enjoy one another's company as mates would, before all hell would be unleashed the following morning when the battle resumed.

It epitomised the spirit of the Ashes in that era. Going back to that 1979–80 tour, when I first spent time with and against DK, Ian Chappell, Greg Chappell, Rod Marsh and the rest, whatever the challenges faced on the field, there was that great tradition at the end of each and every day where players would get together in the fielding side's rooms and share a beer. It was at times like that, and only by that practice, that friendships were established and one got to know one's enemy. It turned out that one's enemy was not only human but in most cases a bloody good human too!

They were – and are – treasured times: eye-opening, educational, inspirational. To have played against the great DK Lillee and to have got to know the man behind the legend is a privilege.

Nowadays the legend even collects and drinks some of Australia's finest wines. I didn't think he could go up in my estimation further, but on those grounds alone he does. Especially when he feels like sharing!

David Gower, former captain of England, 117 Tests

THE BEST OF MY ERA

THE HARDEST PART ABOUT PICKING A 'DREAM Team' of the best players I ever played with or against is not who to put in but who to leave out. It's entirely subjective, and I figure you could ask any of the leading players from my era the same question and they'd all come up with a different team.

This is a list of players I rate as the best during my time only, because I think it's impossible to compare players from different eras. I'm a bit nervous doing this (and that's perhaps why I was never a selector) but here goes: Barry Richards, Gordon Greenidge, Viv Richards, Ian Chappell (captain), Greg Chappell, Gary Sobers, Rod Marsh (and Alan Knott), Andy Roberts, Jeff Thomson, John Snow, and Ashley Mallett.

The only absolute must inclusion is **Garfield Sobers.** In his 93 Test matches Sobers scored 8032 runs at 57.78 including 26 centuries, took 235 wickets at a cost of 34.03 runs apiece and grabbed 109 catches. Include his first-class statistics and you end up with more than 28,000 runs, 86 centuries, 1043 wickets and 407 catches. Sobers's ability to bowl pace and spin with equal efficiency, and his panther-like presence fielding in the covers, made him a captain's dream and virtually provided a team with 12 men in one.

But including Sobers means that many magnificent all-rounders like Ian Botham,

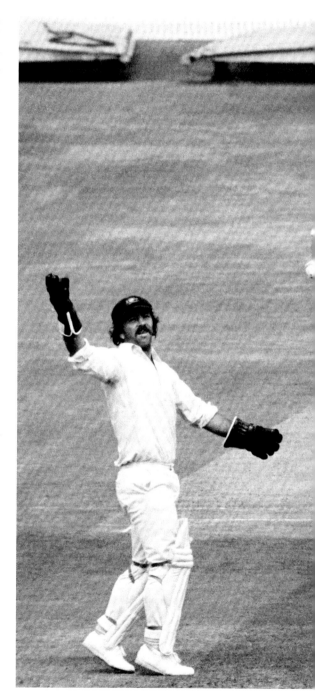

Rod Marsh and Ian Chappell, respectively the best wicketkeeper and captain of my era. I feel unbelievably lucky to have been on the same team.

Richard Hadlee, Imran Khan, Kapil Dev, Mike Procter, Clive Rice and Gary Gilmour don't get a look in. This stuff is hard! It also felt excruciating to omit Michael Holding and Joel Garner, or to believe Malcolm Marshall was fifth cab off the rank when the West Indies toured Australia with their 'fab four' in the late 1970s and early 1980s. I agonised over leaving some of the Australian batsmen I played alongside out of my team. I hope they don't take it personally.

At the head of the order, I picked **Barry Richards**. I didn't bowl to him in Tests because South Africa were in the cricket wilderness in the apartheid era, but Barry's performance in the Sheffield Shield and World Series Cricket really was the stuff of champions. I was one of Western Australia's bowlers on the receiving end when Barry blasted his triple century for South Australia in Perth. Foolishly, as it turned out, our slips cordon got excited that morning when Graham McKenzie beat Richards with the first ball he bowled him. That was the last time a delivery passed his bat.

The best word to describe **Gordon Greenidge** was 'butcher'. When he got going, he would carve any attack to shreds. There was a certain amount of arrogance about how Greenidge operated – bowlers learned to assume absolutely nothing whenever he walked to the crease with a limp, because for some peculiar reason that's when he was at his most ferocious.

Viv Richards was simply the best over the long period he played, and we had some almighty stoushes along the way. I valued

taking his wicket more than any other batsman's, and bowling him for two to have the West Indies reeling at 4–10 in the MCG Test in 1981–82 is forever etched in my mind.

Ian Chappell and **Greg Chappell** have earned their place in my team not simply because they're Australians, but because of their quality. But they were vastly different in how they went about their work, and how they batted was reflected in their captaincies. Greg was a purist, and because he was close to perfection, perfection is what he expected from those in his team right throughout a game. Ian, on the other hand, was more belligerent and unorthodox at the wicket. The philosophy he instilled in the teams he captained was, 'Do it your own way. I don't care how you get it done, just make sure you do.'

And to prove I am not totally parochial, I have bracketed **Rod Marsh** and England's **Alan Knott** as my wicketkeepers. Knott, like Marsh was a superb gloveman. If the crunch came, however, I would go for Rod because of the wonderful rapport we had on the field, his superior batting ability along with his tactical mind. And he was a great captain whenever he got the opportunity.

Picking the fast bowlers was the hardest part, but I simply couldn't overlook **Andy Roberts**. He was the most all-round express bowler who played in my time, and his ability to both attack and defend was his forte. Andy had the ability to 'change up' and bowl exactly according to the condition of the pitch, realising there was no point in bowling at 160kph if the ball was coming on to a batsman beautifully. He had a top outswinger and a good off cutter, which was really a very fast off spinner. Andy also had two bouncers: quick and quicker. During a Supertest at the Sydney Showground, David Hookes painfully discovered the price you paid if you got it wrong hooking Andy. He retired on 81 with a smashed jaw.

Jeff Thomson was the fastest bowler I ever saw, and the reason I loved bowling with him so much was because we fired each other up. It was not something we ever discussed walking out onto the field because we never knew which one of us was going to fire on any particular day. I know I got quite a few of my wickets because batsmen were glad to get away from Thommo.

And, as a pure strike bowler, **John Snow** was without peer. Ray Illingworth knew exactly how to use Snow, and his 28 Test wickets in Australia during the summer of 1970–71 gave England both the edge and the Ashes. Illingworth would use Snow in short, sharp spells, invariably to break a troublesome partnership. It was uncanny how well Illingworth knew Snow and how massively he depended on him – and Snow rarely let his skipper down.

Having moved from Perth to Adelaide in 1967 to benefit from the wisdom of Clarrie Grimmett, I came across **Ashley Mallett**, the best spinner I'd ever seen. His beautiful high-arm action earned him 132 wickets from 38 Tests, and all up his off spinners earned him 693 first-class scalps. He could bowl on any surface; he toured England three times, and

he also found Indian conditions to his liking, out-bowling India's greats Bishan Bedi and Erapalli Prasanna on the 1969 tour of India. And no finger spinner has done better in Australia than his Test best of 8–59 from 23.6 overs against Pakistan at the Adelaide Oval in 1972–73. Although he was short-sighted, some of the catches Mallett plucked in the gully were freakish.

After picking my team, I wondered who my old captain Ian Chappell would choose. I was pleasantly surprised and relieved that we had a big overlap (not to mention thrilled to be included in his team). Ian came up with: Sunil Gavaskar, Barry Richards, Viv Richards, Graeme Pollock, Greg Chappell, Garfield Sobers (captain), Rod Marsh, Andy Roberts, Dennis Lillee, John Snow, Ashley Mallett and Jeff Thomson (12th man).

For the record, I didn't include Graeme Pollock or Sunil Gavaskar in my team because I barely played against Pollock, and Gavaskar never really went well against me. (And not, as you might suspect, because his hissy fit slightly overshadowed me equalling Richie Benaud's Australian record for most wickets!) Sunil was obviously one of the greatest opening batsmen of all time. ◓

OPPOSITE TOP: Opening bat, 'the butcher' Gordon Greenidge at The Oval in London

OPPOSITE BOTTOM: Bev Congdon of New Zealand tries to avoid a bouncer from peerless England bowler John Snow at Trent Bridge, 1973. It might have helped if you'd kept your eyes open, Bev!

TOP: Opening batsman, South African Barry Richards, here being applauded after scoring an undefeated 325, one of the most amazing innings of all time, in a Sheffield Shield match against Western Australia at the WACA in 1970.

CENTRE: In my opinion the most all-round express bowler, Andy Roberts of the West Indies bowling against Australia in Melbourne, 1975.

BOTTOM: What a great photo! That's Greg Chappell batting at The Oval in drizzle in London, 1977. He was just about the perfect batsman (whatever the conditions) and he's batting here with another of my dream team players, Jeff Thomson, the fastest bowler I ever saw.

The psychology of the fast bowler

Dennis was a massive influence during my career and his advice, guidance and support will always be remembered and appreciated. In a quirky sort of way, it was a proud moment for me to go past his record, then beat Ian Botham's record (383 wickets) and then become the first bowler to capture 400 Test wickets.

We had some interesting battles on the field. In 1977, New Zealand were playing Australia at Eden Park in Auckland. New Zealand were in some difficulty at 31/5 in the second innings. Dennis had 4–19 in an inspiring spell of fast bowling. I went to the crease, facing a hat-trick and without a great deal of confidence.

Dennis was bearded and looked mean as he ran in from 30 metres – hard and fast, straight at the batsman. He bowled the ball at 90mph (145kph), which gave the batsman 0.4 of a second to react and play a shot at the ball (even less time if you wanted to change your mind).

I got off the mark with a very fluent off drive to fine leg – a rather thick inside edge or French cut! Within an over or so, I managed to hit one in the middle of the bat – the execution and timing of the shot was to perfection, sending the ball sailing over Dennis's head and into the number one stand for six.

I was very happy with the shot but quickly realised that Dennis had ended up just two metres from me on his follow through. He applauded the shot and I acknowledged him in return saying, 'Thank you, Sir!'

With his fingers he then proceeded to cross me between the eyes as a target for his next delivery. I realised how stupid I had been to put him away for six. I had time to think about the situation I was now in and contemplated what a fast bowler who had just been hit for six might be thinking.

I used to bowl a bit, so I had an idea about what would be going through his mind. It would be too obvious to send down a bouncer to show his annoyance and aggression. I thought that Dennis, being the intelligent Australian that he was, would use reverse psychology and pitch the ball up, to take me unaware and knock my stumps out of the ground. It was, as I expected, pitched up and in the slot. I whacked it over mid-wicket for four runs.

I had hit a six and a four from consecutive deliveries from the great man.

Friendly rivalry. Richard Hadlee indicates with his index finger that he will get me out – which he probably did!

I was then extremely grateful to hear the umpire say, 'That's the end of the over, gentlemen,' to get me out of a very difficult situation, as I was only too aware that I was probably not going to be the eventual winner from the situation that was developing.

As it turned out we lost the Test by an innings, but I managed to score 87, my highest Test score at that time. I was eventually bowled by Greg Chappell when I attempted a big shot and hit across the line of the ball.

Sir Richard Hadlee, 86 Tests for New Zealand

ALLAN LAMB

No quarter given

I first met Dennis in 1982 during the Ash-es tour of Australia. The first Test match was at Perth, his home ground, with his bowling partner Thomson.

Australia have always not walked, so England had a meeting before the Test and decided to play the same way as the Australians and wait for the umpire to give us out.

Well, the Test match got underway, and it was not long before I got to the crease and I was greeted by Rod Marsh, trying to rile me by asking if I had any family, which I ignored. But taking guard, I looked up to see the greatest fast bowler, Dennis Lillee, about to start his run-up from the sightscreen.

The first couple of deliveries I played and missed. When he bowled the fourth ball, which I missed again, he ended up right next to me and flicked the sweat off his forehead and onto my face. It smelled of Bundaberg Rum, DK's favourite tipple. He looked at me and said, 'Hey, mate, do me a favour and hold the bat still and I will aim at the fucking thing,' and walked off.

Not long after I got a blatant nick, the ball went straight to Marsh and they all appealed. DK ran past me and told me to piss off. But I decided to wait for the umpire to give me out, as this was a done thing in Oz. I walked down the wicket to tap down the divot mark, and as I looked up at the umpire, he said, 'Not out!'

I said, 'Great decision, Sir.' But it wasn't long before I was surrounded by Australians telling me exactly what they thought of me.

After each day of play, it was a tradition for the batting side to go into the fielding side's dressing room. Feeling slightly uncomfortable at what happened on the field, I reluctantly went in for a drink. As I walked in, DK shouted, 'Hey, Lamby, come and sit here!' – between DK and Thommo! After a few beers, DK turned round to me and asked if I nicked the delivery that he bowled. I replied, 'Yes, just a faint one, mate.' From that moment, DK and I became great friends and we still are.

Allan Lamb, 79 Tests for England

Although I seemed to have a bit of a reputation for drinking, I rarely actually drank at all. It wasn't that I was against it; I just didn't particularly enjoy beer. Here I am relaxing with an old-fashioned 'shandy' after an exhausting series.

9

WINDING DOWN

When I felt myself slowing with age, I trained harder to try and compensate. But eventually the moment comes when you know it's time to retire.

A guard of honour by the Australian team and about to be congratulated by Greg Chappell; we'd both announced our retirement during a Test against Pakistan at the SCG. Rod Marsh followed suit at the end of the game. It was the ending of an era.

HANGING UP THE BAGGY GREEN

IAN CHAPPELL ALWAYS SAID THAT A PLAYER nearing the end should never listen to the advice or opinions of others – that you alone can make the decision and know when the time is right. I had never taken much notice, to be honest. But as I patrolled the boundary early in the 1983–84 season against Pakistan, I realised he was dead right.

Suddenly it was clear: *I've had enough. I've got to get out of here.*

I made my mind up on the spot that the series would be my last, and that I would tell nobody apart from Helen until just before my last Test in Sydney. There were several factors at play, not least being the fact that my sons were now of an age when they really needed a dad at home rather than continually travelling.

Deep down I knew that I didn't have much time left in the game. Unsettling things began occurring: for instance, in the Brisbane Test of that summer I was brought on as a second change bowler (with the shine well off the ball) behind Geoff Lawson, Rodney Hogg and Carl Rackemann.

I also didn't want to risk breaking down again and facing a long rehabilitation from a back or knee injury. Then there was the media, who had sensed the end was nigh and were picking away like vultures, making my life a misery. While my time playing first-class cricket wasn't over (a few years later I would take up offers to play in Tasmania and in Northamptonshire), I was ready to end this stage of my career.

So, after a win in the first Test at the WACA and consecutive draws in Brisbane, Adelaide and Melbourne (that yielded another 12 wickets), I delicately informed captain Greg Chappell the day before Sydney. He didn't say much beyond, 'Are you sure? It's your decision.' I then told Rod Marsh, who totally understood.

Then events started moving very quickly. At the end of the first day's play, Greg stunned everyone, especially me, when he announced it would be his last Test. I followed suit and called a press conference at the end of day two. Then Rod completed the hat-trick, and at stumps on day three, the assembled cricket writers found themselves interviewing another retiree.

As if buoyed by our decisions, the three of us all made significant contributions in a win for Australia. I followed my first innings 4–65 with 4–88, including the scalp of wicketkeeper Wasim Bari with the very last ball I bowled in Test cricket.

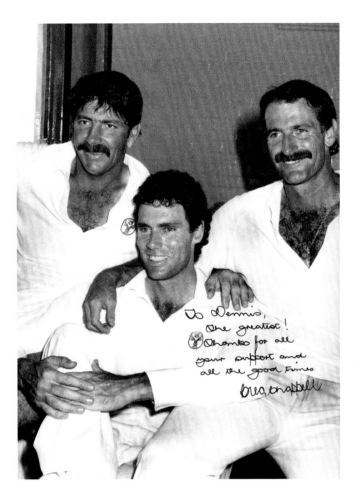

LEFT: Greg gave this signed photo to me in appreciation of our time together as teammates and friends.

BOTTOM: At the MCG after the motorcade. Rod is in one-day gear as he didn't retire from one-dayers until the end of the season. Greg and I retired from both one-dayers and Tests at the same time.

Greg, who always had a sense of occasion, bowed out with a first innings score of 182 to match the 108 he made on debut against England in Perth during the 1970–71 season.

And Rod took five second innings catches to finish with 355 Test dismissals, which was, incredibly, the exact same number of wickets I managed in my 70 Test matches.

When he took the edge offered by Abdul Qadir, it was the 95th time in Tests that a dismissal was recorded as 'caught Marsh, bowled Lillee' – and the last. As the umpire raised his finger it seemed like it had been much longer than 13 years since that day at the SCG when England's John Hampshire, after reaching 10, became the first victim of the productive Lillee–Marsh combination.

Having all made our Test debuts during

the 1970–71 series against England – first Rod in Brisbane, then Greg in Perth and myself in Adelaide – it somehow seemed appropriate that we bow out at the same time although it was never planned that way.

Our amazing cricketing journey together had taken us to places and into situations we could not have envisaged, and our smiles that night were those of three contented men. ●

OPPOSITE: Posing for the camera with Rod and Greg at the end of our last Test. The SCG, 1984.

ABOVE: On our retirement, Greg, Rod and I were given a motorcade around the 'G', much to the appreciation of the Melbourne fans with whom I was lucky to share many career highlights.

AROUND AUSTRALIA

WE MIGHT AS WELL HAVE BEEN DRIVING TO the moon the morning we pulled out of the driveway on our way to explore Australia; we were that excited.

I had long yearned for such a trip, but because of cricketing and business commitments, rehabilitation from injury and trying to maximise normal family time in Perth, I barely had time to take an unscheduled drive around the block. Cricket had taken me to some fantastic places and I'd stayed in some swish hotels, but at the end of my playing career I just wanted to immerse myself in the great outdoors of Australia.

We took Adam and Dean out of school on the understanding that the trip would be educational. In my rush of enthusiasm, I kind of blanked out a few obstacles and challenges that lay ahead. For starters, we'd never been camping before, and the only time I had pitched a tent was during cadet training at school. On top of that, we only had a week to buy a suitable four-wheel drive vehicle and a whole range of camping equipment, including a tent that we hadn't even taken out of the box when we left.

We made it to Geraldton the first day but we took the easy option and spent the first night in a motel because everything had been so rushed (or because I chickened out). We got serious the next day and drove to Monkey Mia, setting up our tent on the dead-calm shores of Shark Bay. We had a great day spent with the boys in the water, interacting with the dolphins (which was allowed then).

Everything was going smoothly, and I began to feel at one with the outdoors, figuring that I was a natural – until I realised the next morning that I'd bogged the bloody car! Just as I wondered how on earth I was going to extricate myself from this embarrassing dilemma, a bloke in a four-wheel drive drove up and offered me some assistance.

To my great surprise, this good Samaritan had no legs. Nevertheless, that didn't affect his agility or mobility, and pretty soon he had us on our way again. He and his mates watched on, shaking their heads at the prospect of me taking my family four-wheel driving through our vast and rugged country.

Perhaps motivated by not wanting people to recognise me when we got into embarrassing situations, and generally just wanting to be incognito for a while, I shaved off all my hair and moustache and went full commando.

My manager, John Cornell, and Paul Hogan were in Darwin filming the original *Crocodile Dundee*, so I decided to pop around to their hotel and put my new look to the test. I knocked on Cornell's door and he looked at me like I was delivering room service to the wrong room. Things were looking promising. I tried Hogan's room and he just opened the door and said, 'G'day Dennis, how ya goin'?' So much for the disguise.

TOP LEFT: On our family trip around Australia in 1985. Bogged on Cape York Peninsula without much help and no trees in sight to set up the winch. Luckily we were dragged out before nightfall and before our fuel ran out.

TOP RIGHT: The sign says it all. At Bamaga, about as far from Perth as it gets while still on the mainland.

ABOVE: Makeshift fish-cleaning station on holidays. Dean, left, and Adam were happy to watch on.

LEFT: Dean and I posing with some Aboriginal rock art.

Retired from cricket and taking a holiday, I decided to shave off all the hair on my head in order to go incognito. But it didn't fool Paul Hogan, who was in Darwin filming the original Crocodile Dundee.

It didn't matter when we got into the more remote parts because there was nobody around, and we were able to enjoy some wonderful times and scenery almost by ourselves. It was incredible – until, as luck would have it, we were in the middle of nowhere in the Northern Territory and I realised we were becoming dangerously low on fuel.

We came across the residence of a station manager and I asked him if I could buy petrol. I lingered a bit, wishing for once that I'd get recognised, but he gave me nothing. I asked him where we might camp, and he just pointed us in the direction of a nearby creek. The next morning I bumped into the same guy and he told me I could buy as much petrol as I liked!

He must have worked out who I was, and he let me know that had I identified myself the previous evening we could have slept in some accommodation that was empty. We declined their new-found hospitality, which included scones, jam, cream and coffee, so we could be on our way in that absolute wilderness. We gradually pushed on all the way to the top of the Cape York Peninsula with the road so rough and rocky we were able to travel only 22 kilometres in about eight hours of rock-hopping. On the return trip from Bamaga, unfortunately a workman's vehicle did a U-turn on the gravel road, collecting us on the rear passenger door. No one was injured, just a little shaken, but the vehicle was worse for wear. Luckily it was still driveable, albeit sucking in dust for the rest of the journey.

On heading south again, we pitched our tent in the Daintree National Park north of Port Douglas. During the night we were caught in a torrential downpour that resulted in our mattresses floating about inside the tent. To add to our discomfort, one of our boys was vomiting uncontrollably, which is not much fun inside a soggy tent.

I have to admit, that's when I waved the white flag, and very early that morning we headed for the sanctuary of a Cairns motel. After a thorough clean and dry, the tent didn't come out of the car again until we reached Perth. We didn't have the expertise of the Leyland brothers, but it was definitely a memorable trip all the same. ●

Our camping skills have improved somewhat since that first trip in 1983, although we are still equally in awe of Australia and, as you can see, still very capable of getting bogged from time to time. Here we are enjoying the Pilbara.

A final year at Northamptonshire

One of the most aggressive bowlers and fiercest competitors of all time on the field, Dennis Lillee is also one of the kindest, most generous and most thoughtful of men off the field. I was teaching at King's Wimbledon in 1988, and my wife, Jane, had an 80-year-old aunt of Scottish descent who had decided to make her first ever trip from Australia to the UK, wanting to trace some of her roots. Dennis was playing his final season of cricket at the time at Northamptonshire. Jane was to drive her Aunt Fon from Wimbledon to Scotland, and she arranged to break the journey and stay overnight with Dennis.

Not a close follower of sport, Fon was not at all keen to meet and stay with Dennis. She had formed the view that he was an aggressive ruffian. Though Jane reassured her, Fon remained wary. Dennis provided a right royal welcome when they arrived that evening, immediately providing hot tea and cake. After they had freshened up with a shower, he provided the ladies with a couple of gin and tonics. These preceded perfectly cooked roast lamb and a bottle of red wine. Much storytelling, teasing and laughter followed, along with a nightcap. Fon and Jane arose the next morning and walked out to a large cooked breakfast. They drove off after hugs and fond farewells and 15 hours full of kindness and joy, with Fon saying, 'If I ever hear one of my friends say a bad word about Dennis Lillee I shall hit them over the head with my walking stick.' Fon came to love him, as all who know him do.

John Inverarity, six Tests for Australia, former captain of Western Australia and former chairman of selectors for Cricket Australia

This was my second game for Northamptonshire in 1988. I went over on my ankle while quickly changing direction when fielding. I tore most of the ligaments and tendons in my ankle as well as cracking a bone. With heaps of intensive physio and hard work, I was playing again in six or seven weeks (though not at my best). I wish I could have played the whole season, as it was an enjoyable time at the club and they were a top lot of people.

My action still looked to be in pretty good shape at Northamptonshire in 1988.

OPENING WITH ADAM

FOUND MYSELF UNDER PRESSURE SEVERAL times during my Test career, but I reckon the Chairman's XI v Pakistan at Perth's Lilac Hill in 1999 – long after I had retired from the international arena – topped the lot.

At the age of 50, and having informed officials that it would be my last Lilac Hill game, I asked if our 25-year-old son, Adam, could share the new ball bowling duties with me. Even though Adam had only just started playing again after several years off, I thought he was pretty handy.

While driving to Lilac Hill with Adam that morning, I asked him if he was nervous. He said that bowling to Test batsmen would be a bit daunting, but he wasn't nervous – meanwhile I was nervous as hell. (Actually, I was nervous before every game throughout my whole career.)

At first, the Lilac Hill organisers hadn't been terribly excited about Adam playing but they went along with it and benefited from a fair bit of pre-match publicity. And wouldn't you know – after four overs, Pakistan had slumped to 2–9 and Adam had taken both wickets.

For the first time in my life I had opted to bowl into the breeze and let Adam enjoy its benefits. I clearly still had my work cut out for me in making up the leeway in this friendly (but still a little bit serious) rivalry.

Then a most extraordinary thing happened: I dropped a delivery in short

to opener Ghulam Ali, and he obliged by hooking it high and handsomely in the direction of Adam at fine leg. Because shots like that in grade cricket rarely travel the full distance, Adam overran it. Suddenly he began rapidly back-pedalling towards the boundary. At the same time, he frantically stuck his right hand high above his head and, to his disbelief, the ball stuck firmly in his palm. It was an amazing catch, and the big crowd erupted. I raced to embrace my son who was, naturally, grinning from ear to ear.

Adam went on to dismiss Yousuf Youhana (Mohammad Yousuf) to make his haul three wickets to my one. I ended up with two more, including that of Shoaib Akhtar with my last delivery in cricket, which was a nice little echo of my last delivery in Test cricket, with which I dismissed Pakistan's Wasim Bari.

An unforgettable day had finished with Adam taking 3–29 off six overs, while I had 3–8 from eight. And, on the strength of his performance, Adam was immediately promoted to first grade.

One of the boys from the press box overheard an old English journalist, who was covering the Pakistan tour for a London newspaper, dictating his story on the match. The journalist began his piece by saying, 'The news from Australia is getting bleaker by the day – there is now a Lillee bowling from both ends.' ●

Playing my last game with our eldest son, Adam. What a thrill! We played against Pakistan at Lilac Hill on 26 October 1999, and it was my last official cricket match at any level. Adam and I took three wickets apiece, and I got Shoaib Akhtar with the last ball I ever bowled in a match.

Coaching in India with the MRF (Madras Rubber Factory) Pace Foundation.

10

COACHING

I'd never considered coaching, and had always thought my love of cricket was confined to playing the game. But after a stint in New Zealand and an opportunity in India, coaching provided a new lease on my cricket life.

KEEPING PACE

IHADN'T THOUGHT ABOUT GOING INTO COACHING until New Zealand asked me to help some of their teenage talent after I retired from playing. I enjoyed that experience so much that I was then open to a suggestion from the Madras Rubber Factory (MRF), one of the biggest companies in the southern hemisphere, to establish a fast bowling foundation in India. Ravi Mammen was the dynamo behind this idea. I went to meet him in Chennai and we got along so well that I took on the challenge.

We started from scratch, and the first few years were shambolic – although a mostly enjoyable shambles. MRF was one of the most ethical and supportive groups I've ever had the pleasure of working with, and that was the key to our perseverance and subsequent success. We built it up methodically and painstakingly, and expanded to coaching international cricketers as well as cricket coaches themselves. It was very hard work, but I'm confident that the MRF Pace Foundation is one of the finest facilities in the world dedicated to the art of fast bowling.

I had 25 very happy years popping over to India regularly, and I was delighted when one of our former alumni, the great Glenn McGrath, took over from me as director in 2012. I've also thoroughly enjoyed my stints working with the WACA, New Zealand, the old Australian Cricket Board and, more recently, Cricket Australia. That's probably about it for me coaching now, though – in an official capacity, at least – but I'm still more than happy to work with individual bowlers, which has always been the most fulfilling part of coaching.

I was privileged in my career to be mentored by some of the best cricket coaches and players in the game, and so it's been my pleasure to pass on the knowledge that I've gained. Of course to be useful you have to keep learning yourself, and it was in the course of my coaching that I began to fully realise how little we knew about technique and training in my playing days.

I distinctly remember trying to work it all out for myself, which, I suppose, is a good experience for a coach. For example, at the end of play in state games, John Inverarity and I, sometimes along with Rod Marsh, would go to the outside broadcasting vans parked around the WACA. We would ask the television technicians to replay the tapes of us slowly so that we could try and work out what we were doing wrong or could do better. Coming from that, the digital technology we take for granted today is amazing.

Our understanding of fast bowling is evolving all the time. There's definitely a competitive edge to be gained by whichever team is most dedicated to mastering the art. As seen throughout the history of cricket,

Giving pointers to a young James Brayshaw. There is only so much a coach can do!

having strike bowlers playing at the top of their game is one of the most effective and, for fans, most enjoyable ways of winning matches.

For me, the most satisfying aspects of coaching were working with established bowlers trying to finesse their action and attitude so they could get the most out of their natural attributes, as well as spotting the raw talent in kids who might not be getting the best out of themselves but who have the natural mechanics that could make them the next Glenn McGrath or Mitchell Johnson. ●

Snapshots from my time with the MRF Pace Foundation.

CLOCKWISE FROM TOP LEFT: From the humble beginnings pictured here, I'm proud that so many great cricketers came to and through the MRF Pace Foundation during my long and enjoyable stint there; Shoaib Akhtar of Pakistan (with the MRF Pace Foundation facility in the background); our own Brett Lee; Joel Garner of the West Indies (centre) and Henry Olanga of Zimbabwe (right); two great friends and the main men behind MRF Pace Foundation, Mr Rathnam (left) and TA Sekar (right); Lance Klusener of South Africa; and Javagal Srinath of India.

DK in India

Around 1986 I came to know that Dennis Lillee was interested in associating with our company, MRF, on a project to develop fast bowlers. Being a cricket fan myself and having always followed Dennis – seeing him as an aggressive and dominant bowler – I was wondering how we would be able to convince him to coach the Indian bowlers when we didn't even have a facility yet.

We started using a local cricket field with only a few selected trainees, and Dennis's approach was clinical from the outset. He focused on attitude, action, physical conditioning and mental preparation: all key attributes for any fast bowler. And it became obvious pretty soon that a key attribute for the Foundation was a proper facility.

Some people think bowling is just about delivering the ball to get the batsman out, but that requires a great deal of mental and physical preparation at each and every stage – selecting the right candidate, setting up an appropriate gym, developing the best action, taking care of diet, devising training schedules, match practice, video analysis and, above all, mental conditioning to be able to bowl quickly, accurately and consistently.

That was the groundwork the great Dennis Lillee started us on. He had the curators prepare the four or five types of pitches needed to simulate the various conditions bowlers would encounter internationally. We had to recruit a team of experts for each activity, including a translator to interpret Dennis's Australian English into Indian English, Hindi and several other local languages for the assorted trainees.

TA Sekar, who had played for India, was the chief coach, interpreting the skills of Dennis Lillee by systematically evolving a perfect coaching syllabus. From humble beginnings, which were more about passion than pragmatism, the results are clear. Many world-class bowlers have graduated from the Pace Foundation, including Australians Glenn McGrath, Brett Lee and Shane Watson, New Zealander Tim Southee and many other bowlers from just about every cricketing nation.

Dennis Lillee's ability to translate bowling into a scientific practice – from inside and outside the boundary line – is amazing. The MRF Pace Foundation continues the good work pioneered by Dennis, now with another Australian legend: its former student Glenn McGrath. And yes, we still require the translator for Glenn.

SR Rathnam, former director in charge of the MRF Pace Foundation

Light days at the MRF Pace Foundation

Hard work was something I got a rude introduction to, aged 14, at the MRF Pace Foundation. According to Dennis, sir, this was the very foundation of the hardest job in cricket – fast bowling.

The message was clear the first time Dennis spoke to the lucky few who had been selected for MRF Pace in 2005: if he was going to invest his time and energy in us, we had better guarantee him that we were going to work our backsides off. And trust me, it wasn't the place to make an idle promise. I knew Dennis meant business because every year I would see the guys who were a little slack being sent home.

One of Dennis's most dreaded methods of seeing if we were at our top fitness was to make us do a 5 kilometre time trial after a long session of bowling in the sweltering Chennai heat. Anything over 19 mins was too slow. And this would usually happen after he'd start the morning by saying, 'Boys, today is going to be a light day!'

I had no idea back then just how valuable the lessons Dennis gave me were. I remember him telling me how stress fractures nearly ended his career but he never let it get him down. Instead, he worked on his action, trained even harder and came back as a better bowler. He had such an impact on the way I think and on my basic beliefs about the game. See, I have suffered six stress fractures in my spine in the span of the last eight years, and the only reason I have come back every time and bowled as fast as I still do is because of Dennis, sir. If I hadn't bought into his ideals of determination, dedication and discipline, and put

Varun Aaron bowling for India in 2014.

in those hard yards, I might not be playing cricket now. He still remains a massive figure of inspiration for me and, I'm sure, for many other fast bowlers in India who he has touched in his 25 years at the MRF Pace Foundation. His contribution to me as a cricketer and to Indian fast bowling is invaluable, and I am determined to do him proud by the time I hang up my boots.

Varun Aaron, 7 Tests for India

Young Indian batsman gets hold of DK

In 1999, Dennis and Helen invited my wife, Von, and I to join them in India for a couple of weeks.

After a few days at leisure in frenetic Chennai, we had the opportunity to go to the opening day of an historic Test match: the first match between India and Pakistan since the border war between those two major, nuclear-armed powers a decade earlier. This was a *big* event that, not surprisingly, was surrounded by strict security. The four of us – Dennis, Helen, Von and I – were guests of MRF, but of course we had to go through security like everybody else.

This involved being frisked by heavily armed security staff. The security staff for our particular search were very tall and handsome Sikh soldiers and, embarrassingly for both Dennis and me, Helen and Von insisted on going through the frisking process *twice*, stating that the soldiers may have missed something the first time around!

Inside the impressive Chennai stadium, the atmosphere was tense, but the capacity crowd was strangely subdued, at least initially. Perhaps the armed Indian soldiers along the boundary line had something to do with that.

Between Tests, we enjoyed the beautiful, white-sand beaches of Goa. In India you see kids playing cricket everywhere with anything that resembles a ball and a bat. As we walked along the beach one day, a tennis ball from one of these games landed near us. Instinctively, Dennis collected it and began his unmistakable rhythmic approach to the 'crease'.

The ball was a pretty fair one, albeit not at full pace. The junior batsman, not recognising the bowler and completely unfazed, danced down the 'wicket' and unceremoniously hoisted the delivery from one of the finest fast bowlers ever to play the game a good 75 metres to square leg and into the rolling surf! Not surprisingly, Dennis declined to fetch the ball, although I think it was one time he didn't mind a batsman getting hold of him.

A few days later, as we wandered anonymously through a fishing village, we noticed that radios and tiny black-and-white television sets were tuned in to the second India–Pakistan Test match. India was fielding and Anil Kumble was bowling – but not only was he bowling, he was working his way towards the momentous achievement of taking all 10 wickets in an innings.

People huddled over their radios and crowded around the few television sets. The atmosphere was electric, but hushed. There was not the roar of a capacity crowd at the MCG with Lillee steaming in and Bay 13 in uproar: this was a nation holding its breath. Dennis paused as the final few wickets fell to the wily spinner, with the huddled fishermen and their families oblivious to his presence. In the course of the next half-hour, Kumble achieved the ultimate (10 for 74), and the whole place erupted!

Michael Bromilow, friend

Here I am around 2008 in the XXXX Gold Beach Cricket Competition. A bit older, a bit fuller-bodied, a bit less expansive in the delivery stride and certainly not getting the results that I used to. Obviously too old for this caper. In the last year of the event, Thommo and I were retired to promotional activities in the beer tent.

An eye for detail

There is no doubt Dennis was the premier fast bowler in world cricket for a decade or more. Since his retirement from Test cricket in 1984, he has spent more than two decades coaching fast bowlers and more than a decade attempting to sort out the Western Australian Cricket Association (WACA).

For over 20 years, he went to India to the MRF Pace Foundation where he resided over the development of young Indian fast bowlers. The story goes that even a young Sachin Tendulkar came along to see if he could develop his fast bowling skills! It's a shame for bowlers all over the world that Dennis didn't accept him into the fast bowling program.

Dennis understands the mechanics of fast bowling and communicates the basics very well. In my role as head of the Australian Cricket Academy in Adelaide, I used DK as a special coach every year and was totally fascinated by what he could see with the naked eye – I battled to pick up the salient points on slow-motion video.

One incident at the academy springs to mind immediately. Jamie Siddons, then captain of South Australia, came to the indoor centre to have a net against some of our fast bowlers. Dennis was supervising the fast bowlers and instructing them on just how to bowl to Jamie. He kept repeating that an off-stump line to Jamie was just too wide and it was pointless bowling anything but a middle and leg line.

Our young fast bowlers kept bowling on or just outside off-stump, and Jamie kept smacking them through the off side. DK said, 'Stand aside,' did a half-hearted

stretch, picked up a ball and bowled a perfect outswinger starting just outside leg stump, finishing on a middle and leg line and catching the edge of Jamie's bat. He turned to the boys and said, 'That's the line I'm talking about.'

Just because you've been a great player doesn't mean you will make a great coach. But just as Dennis was recognised by his peers as the best fast bowler of his time, he was also recognised as being the premier fast bowling coach in world cricket after his retirement from playing.

I never, for one moment, thought DK would become a cricket administrator, but he spent 11 years as president of the WACA. During his reign he attempted to make watching cricket a far more casual affair for the president's guests. Gentlemen were requested not to wear ties, and Dennis tried to enforce this where possible. Because DK is the legend he is, he was able to open doors that others couldn't.

The WACA will certainly miss Dennis as their president, but life goes on. All I know is that there hasn't been a greater influence on West Australian cricket over the last 50 years than DK Lillee. I could probably go one step further and say that, in my opinion, there hasn't been a more influential person in the history of fast bowling.

Rod Marsh, 96 Tests for Australia, chairman of selectors for Cricket Australia and former manager of Elite Coaching Development in Australia, England and India

My great mate Rod Marsh went on to become one of the best coaches in the game and has done so much to foster talent and lift standards throughout the cricketing world.

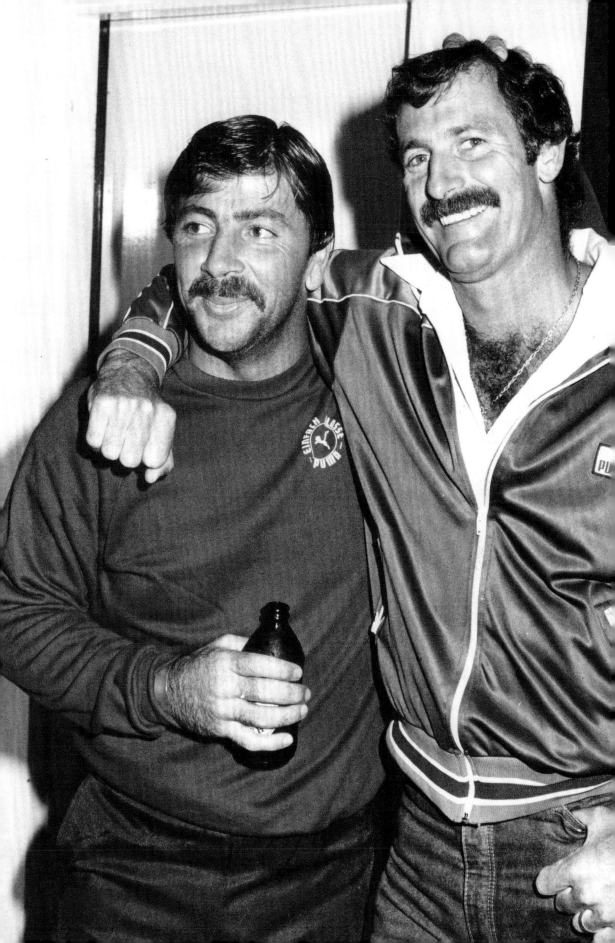

At the WACA in 2010. This marked one of the greatest comebacks from injury (and turnarounds of form) I've seen in a fast bowler. I was delighted to help Mitch find his way again. There are very few fast bowlers who can fill an entire team with apprehension, and Mitch was up there with the best of them.

Getting the most out of Mitch

The first time I properly met Dennis was when I was around 18, during my second year at the Australian Cricket Academy run by Rod Marsh. We were all excited the night before Dennis was coming in to chat to us about fast bowling – doubly excited because it meant that we didn't have training the next morning, so we thought we would stop by a popular nightclub and have a few.

When we arrived at the nightclub, one of the boys mentioned that DK was there. Knowing that my even being at the academy was thanks to Dennis, who saw some potential in me, I set off to buy the great man a drink. When I found him, he said, 'No way, champ.' I was taken aback, and thought maybe he didn't approve of us young blokes drinking while at the academy. But then he said, 'I've got it. When you're playing for Australia, then you can buy me a drink.'

We got chatting about cricket and anything else I could think of, really, and I'm pretty sure the sun was coming up by the time we left. I was woken by my roomy a couple of hours later – and not in a great state. Somehow I got myself together and into the room in time for Rod to inform us that Dennis had been slightly held up. Whoops! All the boys tried to stifle their chuckles.

Half an hour later in came Dennis, and he shot me a look that said, *Wow, big night. Don't tell Rod.* We didn't mention it to Rod, of course, but later we realised that they're such good mates, Rod probably knew exactly what was going on.

> Despite our fairly casual start, I never once took for granted the opportunity to work with one of the greats of Australian cricket – in fact, one of the greats of the game itself.

Spring forward to 2010, the Ashes series at home. I'd been dropped for the second Test in Adelaide. I wasn't happy about it, but all I could do was knuckle down and work as hard as I could to get back on the side for the next Test in Perth. I was working with Troy 'Truck' Cooley (a fast bowling coach and DK's great mate) and Stuart Karppinen (a fitness trainer) in the nets in Adelaide, and they suggested we head to Perth early to do some work with Dennis.

I always felt comfortable working with Dennis because we just got on really well. We all got together in the nets at the Subiaco Floreat ground. Dennis got straight to work, asking about my run-up. We spoke about my run-up many times over my career. It needed to be just right: strong, at the optimum pace. We also worked on my back leg, ensuring I wasn't sitting on it for too long, which was why the run-up was so important. My front arm was the next thing, making sure I was pulling in to my hip then finishing off down past my knee.

Dennis was brilliant for me because he kept it simple and worked to maximise what I had, rather than trying to change me. But it wasn't just technique he helped with: we also talked about being mentally strong, as that was the thing I was trying to focus on most at that time.

Honestly, it was one of the best net sessions I've ever had. I was in such a bad way after being dropped and was so unsure of my action. That time with DK made all the difference. Getting picked for the Perth Test and destroying the England team (I got 6–38) after that session made me realise how lucky I was to have Truck, Stu and DK in my corner.

Mitchell Johnson, 73 Tests for Australia

Ready to listen

What Australian cricket fan didn't try to emulate Dennis Lillee? What a character – with the long hair flapping, the extended run-up, the gold chain and exposed chest, the action that was like poetry in motion, scaring the tripe out of batsmen – and how much he was loving it. But best of all, he was an Aussie!

I first met him when I was 16. I was trying to bowl at 180 clicks to impress him. He called me over and said, 'You've got great pace, son, but if you don't change your action you'll get stress fractures in your lower back.'

I was like, 'Huh?'

'You'll probably break your back.'

And just like most 16-year-olds, even though it was Dennis Lillee, I thought I knew better and ignored his advice. Two and a half years later, I got a stress fracture in my back. I called him up and said, 'Hi, Dennis, it's Brett Lee here. I'm ready to listen.'

Our friendship grew from there, and he became my mentor. I wasn't even playing Shield cricket then and Dennis didn't get a cent for helping me; he did it all off his own bat because that's the type of person he is, a beauty of a bloke. You don't see that in a lot of past players.

Dennis made me the bowler I was, changing my action and my whole approach to the game when it came to training and conditioning. But the way he helped me most was mentally. For starters, how to deal with injury. Unless you've bowled with pain, you can't really appreciate what Dennis did in his career, and I don't think

I've bowled without pain since I was 16 – there's always some sort of niggle. I was inspired by how Dennis dealt with his own pain, and how he evolved as a bowler in the face of injury. He took a few kilometres off his pace and ended up with a beautiful, clean and economical action.

I reckon he is one of the best athletes Australia's ever had, right across sport. Being able to bowl for long spells in extreme summer heat at the MCG, for example, in front of 100,000 fans, *and* take Viv Richards's wicket with the last ball of the day: that's just extraordinary.

He held the record for most Australian Test wickets for a long time, but I think what was so special was the *way* he took the wickets and the absolute carnage he caused. I'm sure other bowlers would have benefitted from having Dennis getting in the heads of the batsmen.

He has been incredibly generous in passing his know-how on to upcoming bowlers like me, and I was like a sponge, always soaking up his wisdom. Not only was he one of the finest fast bowlers ever, he's an amazing character who was good for the game and the fans. I hope characters like him will come through the Australian team in the future, and that they will be just as generous.

Dennis taught me that it's important to pass on what you know – even if you're not the most confident or articulate person. The smallest thing could be the missing piece of the puzzle for someone else.

Brett Lee, 76 Tests for Australia

Like Mitch, Brett's express pace gave many of the world's best batsmen nightmares. His ability to come back from injury time and time again was testament to his character. Here he's bowling in Delhi, India in 2008.

Never book an appointment before noon

I'll never forget Brian Davison, our Tasma-nian skipper, escorting DK out onto the Devonport Oval to introduce our latest import. My life in cricket changed that day, and the privileges I've enjoyed from then have led me to where I am now in this great game. Opening the bowling with Dennis (into the wind, of course) was something most young fast bowlers could only dream of.

I soon became Lillee's 'into-the-wind bowler' as assistant coach, delivering the Pace Australia Program. I was working for the Australian Cricket Academy (under Rod Marsh) as the pace and fitness coach, and it was there I got mentored in the art of coaching fast bowlers.

It was inspirational watching DK. He'd bring the wide-eyed young guns in close, tell them to tighten up closer and then deliver his overriding message: 'Boys, the secret to fast bowling is Hard Work, More Hard Work and More Bloody Hard Work!'

In my first year as his 'assistant', I accompanied him on trips to all the states and territories. My role was to listen, help and take notes for player's reports. I set up all the visits and any extra meetings and coaching seminars the states wanted.

DK never gave less than 100 per cent at his sessions. While he was coaching the players he would make small adjustments to their techniques and talk them through situations that would leave lasting impressions. He could still find the top of off or the glove – or could make it nip back and

hit the pad – to illustrate what he was telling the players. We would work well into the evening, but the players never wanted the sessions to stop. And when he was done with the players, he would coach the coaches. We always found ourselves at a late dinner, or at the bar with the 'mature' players, laying plans for the total destruction of all known batsmen.

As well as the need to work hard, Dennis's other golden rule was to never book a meeting or session before noon – a rule that I didn't take seriously enough when my ex-coach Greg 'Shippy' Shipperd scheduled a meeting at 8am. The taxi ride with Dennis to the Victorian office was decidedly icy, and I thought my role could be in serious jeopardy. I've witnessed FOT's best and worst moods, and have been lucky that the latter were always directed at the opposition. On this particular morning, I got a whiff of what it must have been like at the other end of the pitch. But when we got there Dennis was a champion, as always, and the Vics would never have realised there was a problem; his barbs were very subtle and all aimed at me. At the end of the day, he didn't miss me in delivering a simple message: 'Truck, I will say this once more and once more only – never, ever set up a meeting at this time again.'

I'm pleased to report that I never made the mistake again and, to this day, I never call him before noon.

Troy Cooley, head coach at Cricket Australia's National Performance Program

Above board

I had done a lot of technical work on my action since first working with Dennis in 1991, and I'd found a yard or two of pace, playing mostly for Queensland. But my bowling arc was now 'messy' and the changes to my action had attracted the attention of umpires (and some players) over its legality. This was the season after the incident between Muttiah Muralitharan and Darrell Hair, and I felt like I was getting caught up in the fallout of that episode. No Australian bowler had been queried since Ian Meckiff and, I have to admit, it was pretty traumatic for me.

Simply telling the authorities that I'd sorted out my action was not going to cut it. I needed someone who understood the is-sue, could provide the answers and who had the trust of the decision-makers. The only person was Dennis. I knew I had to catch up with him and sort through the technical stuff or risk the end of my cricket career.

I couldn't get hold of Dennis, but I de-cided to hop on a flight to Perth and hope for the best. On arrival, I got onto Den-nis's son, Adam. He told me his father and mother were on holidays at a fairly remote place south of Perth and that divulging numbers or their exact location would not end well for him. Determined to track Dennis down, I hired a car, bought a map and headed south to the town Adam had mentioned. I drove through the night call-ing Adam each time I got mobile phone coverage. Around midnight I drove into a town and found a place to stay.

The next morning, I got back on the road and checked in again. By this stage,

Adam had taken pity on me and handed over his dad's mobile number. (I'm forever grateful, Adam!) I called Dennis and must have sounded desperate. 'Dennis, I'm in trouble regarding my action and badly need some help. I want to see you so I can sort it out and get organised for the next game.' That next game happened to be in Perth in little over a week!

'Two things, Greg,' said Dennis. 'First, sometimes it takes a long while to change your action, and second, I'm in nearly the most remote part of Western Australia you could think of, and the complete opposite end of the country to you.'

Then I told him where I was and, after a moment's silence, Dennis gave me detailed directions to a small, deserted carpark and told me to wait there. While I waited I noticed a beautiful estuary and wandered over to take in the view. It was a picture-perfect scene as one lonely boat emerged out of the wilderness, the 'skipper' in full holiday mode – beard, hat and sunglasses – with his 'first mate' at the bow. It was only when he turned the tiller to come into the jetty that I realised the deadpan skipper was Dennis himself. He greeted me with a big laugh and told me to throw my stuff in. His mate, Geoff, helped us load in my video gear, bowling kit and everything I needed to show them some video footage and perhaps take some more.

We tootled across the river to a remote residence and found some green space to bowl a few. The run-up was across a dirt road, through a gap in a hedge and onto a

pretty well-manicured lawn. Geoff held the camera and retrieved the balls, and we all retired to the beach shack to check the video. This went on and on, back and forth, until Dennis was onto the issue and the remedial action required.

Doctor Dennis diagnosed my problem as getting too side-on in the delivery stride – what we call 'beyond side-on'. This was compromising my load-up. My bowling arm was coming sharply across my body in an effort to get the ball into a power position for delivery at the target. Further confusing the issue was the fact that I was double-jointed in that arm, so the jerky outcome was not a pretty sight. He wasn't surprised that I'd been told the action was unacceptable. He suggested that I concentrate on bringing my body around in the gather and bringing my bowling arm straight up and down, not across my chest.

With the session over at dusk, we got in the tinny and headed back down the river. We unloaded the gear and I hightailed it back to Perth to get the 'red-eye' over to Brisbane. It was one of the most exhilarating experiences of my life driving back to Perth that day – the sun setting over the Indian Ocean on the left, the changing colours of the West Australian landscape on the right, and Dennis's support behind and ahead of me.

When I got back to Brisbane, I continued with the remedial work and made a complex submission to Cricket Australia, complete with footage and Dennis's endorsement. I was cleared to play. A week later I was back in Perth, playing for Queensland. Thanks to Dennis, I never had another issue with my action, but this act of generosity from Dennis (and Adam) when the chips were down will stay with me for life.

Greg Rowell, state cricketer for the Queensland Bulls, New South Wales Blues and Tasmanian Tigers

I had great experiences coaching young cricketers like Greg Rowell, Mitchell Johnson, Brett Lee and many others. Here I am with the very talented James Pattinson at the WACA in 2013. I don't think James has reached his full potential yet.

Receiving a framed cap after being inducted into the ICC Hall of Fame during a Test match between Australia and the West Indies at the WACA in 2009. In a way, everything I achieved in cricket happened because of my start at the WACA. It was always most special to celebrate achievements back on my home ground.

DENNIS LILLEE MBE
ICC CRICKET HALL OF FAME
IN ASSOCIATION WITH FICA
2009

PRESENTED BY
ICC DIRECTOR & CRICKET AUSTRALIA CHAIRMAN
JACK CLARKE
DECEMBER 2009 - WACA

11

HOME AT THE WACA

Being from Western Australia and having the WACA as my home venue helped me get selected for Australia. I'm incredibly proud to be a 'sandgroper' and cherish my long association with WA cricket, even when it has come with drama.

PUTTING IN FOR STATE

I'M NOT SURE IF I WOULD EVER HAVE GOT TO play for Australia if I hadn't been from Western Australia. I have never underestimated how much I got from my home state, although I feel confident that I've given back everything I possibly could.

> Conventional wisdom says that my performance for WA against the MCC in Perth, when I turned Geoff Boycott's cap with a lifter and had many batsmen guessing, was what convinced the Australian selectors to put me in the team for my first Test.

The defining moment of my whole cricketing career came at the WACA on 11 December 1971, when we played a Rest of the World team that was touring in place of the banned South Africans. I took a lot of wickets, and we bowled out a quality side for 59; that was a massive boost to my confidence and left a huge impression on me as a young man. No doubt I was helped by the WACA wicket, but I managed to exploit those opportunities. I doubt I could have made the same impact at any other ground in Australia.

I loved playing at the WACA. I had a spe-

cial affinity with the wicket, as well as the crowd. The parochial crowd used to chant, 'Kill, kill, kill,' as I came in off my very long run-up. Sometimes the bar staff would also choose that moment to tap a new keg of beer, so a great hissing noise would add to the effect; this was definitely disconcerting to batsmen. Some batsmen claimed that I herded as many flies as possible into the ground as well, just to put them off!

What's more, I was lucky to play in a great era for West Australian cricket. We won four Shields out of six between 1971 and 1977. Western Australia had six players in the Australian team for most of that period, but we were available to play for our state much more regularly than the top players these days. I know it will sound biased, but I've no doubt, even on mature recollection, that the greater conditioning and camaraderie of the Western Australia team from those days had a very significant impact on the Australia team, who'd been struggling up until then.

Western Australia also won the Shield in 1978, but by that time I was playing World Series Cricket and was, most disappointingly, shunned for that act by many fans, players and especially WA officialdom. Although I made things right with fans and players quickly enough, I had a very cool relationship with WACA officials for many years. That only really ended in 2004, when I was convinced to become president of the WACA at

Western Australia team photo, 1969–70 season. Eight played, or went on to play, Test cricket. Derek Chadwick went on the Australian tour of New Zealand in 1970. Back row: Jock Irvine; DKL; Clark Scarff; Terry Prindiville; Ross Edwards; Tony Mann. Front row: Rod Marsh; Bob Meuleman; Graham McKenzie; Tony Lock; John Inverarity; Derek Chadwick.

a time of struggle for West Australian cricket. I'm sad that after putting in as president for 11 years, and doing my part to help right the ship as it were, things soured again. In 2015 I felt like I had to walk away.

I don't want to go into the detail of the political machinations that are taking place there. To be honest, I don't really feel like I've got the energy for that fight anymore. But I will say that my concern is primarily over the future of the WACA Ground itself. I have a unique relationship with that ground, but I dare say the venue has a special place in the hearts of many Australian and international players and cricket fans. I wish more value was put on the heritage of the place. I am immensely proud, along with my great mate Rod Marsh, to have a stand in our names. I just hope it's still there by the time I cark it. ●

Western Australia players returning home from the tour of the West Indies in 1973. L–R: (in hat) Bob Massie, Ross Edwards, DKL and Rod Marsh.

The view from 'the other end'

I never had the joy of playing Test cricket with FOT, but I did have the privilege of playing with him many times for Western Australia – including in his debut game in Brisbane at the start of the 1969–70 season. Those who were at the Gabba that day witnessed the dawning of a new age for Australian cricket. Here was a young man who could send them down mighty fast, and who from day one demonstrated an admirable contempt for the batsman. Subsequently, too many times to count, I was the real beneficiary of being the bowler 'at the other end'. His presence made it so much easier for us 'lesser lights'.

Dennis grew to be a giant among giants, but on that first tour for WA he was found wanting once he was away from the field of endeavour. One afternoon, the Gabba was flooded by a deluge of amazing proportions. Play was off for the day, and in the paper the next morning was a creative photo showing a beer can on its side half-covered by the deep water on the ground. In the dressing room later, young Dennis was looking at the photo, aghast. 'Jeez, did it rain yesterday ... What about that?! A 44-gallon drum in the outfield, half-covered with water!' Well, we may have enjoyed a laugh then – but it would be the last time. The young quickie was quick to learn, and before the tour was out it was he who was having the fun at others' expense, and he earnt himself a reputation as a great practical joker.

Ian Brayshaw, author, played 101 matches for Western Australia

My West Australian teammates who contributed to Australia's Test successes over many years.

THE MIRACLE MATCH

THE WEST AUSTRALIAN DRESSING ROOM WAS A seething pit at the halfway mark of the one-day game against Queensland at the WACA Ground. It was 12 December 1976, and the star-studded home team had just been bowled out for a seemingly pathetic 77 in a semi-final of the domestic Gillette Cup.

In front of almost 10,000 spectators, Queensland skipper Greg Chappell, with my old mate Jeff Thomson champing at the bit, won the toss, and immediately applied the pressure by asking us to bat. It was a good move, as the wicket looked great to bowl on.

Thommo was thundering in and had Bruce Laird snapped up in the slips for eight, before Ric Charlesworth and Rob Langer took the score to 50. Then Langer was out to Geoff Dymock for 15 and Charlesworth was next for 25 with no addition to the score. What followed was a disaster: Kim Hughes, Craig Serjeant and Rod Marsh all dismissed without scoring. We lost five wickets for one run!

Ian Brayshaw and Bruce Yardley advanced the score to a shaky 76, then yours truly and Wayne Clark took the total of ducks in our innings to five, and 77 was the sum total. Geoff Dymock (3–20), Phil Carlson (3–17) and Greg Chappell (2–3) were the other wicket-takers.

Captain Rod Marsh was inconsolable in the rooms, and lunch was hard to eat. Adding to the pressure, Queensland featured two of the world's best batsmen in Greg Chappell and West Indian superstar Viv Richards. Everyone was thoroughly dejected.

> Marsh, a fiercely proud 'sandgroper', suddenly began pacing up and down the room, getting fired up. Caught in the moment, I yelled out, 'WE *WILL* WIN THIS MATCH!'

Everyone looked at me as though I was crazy, but Marsh took it further. With the tension tight as a drum he said, 'There are three points I want to make. One: a lot of people have paid a lot of money to watch us, and we cannot let them down! Two: I want you to go out there and bowl and field like you never have before, and I want each and every one of you to give 150 per cent!' With that, he charged for the door and yelled, 'Let's go!'

I hadn't realised how brave Ric Charlesworth was until the moment he said, 'Hey, Rod, what was the third point?' The look Marsh gave him could have melted steel.

Viv Richards took strike and I knew I had to get rid of him quickly. I figured if I 'roughed them up' a bit we would either win or get smashed. With so few runs to play with, I had to take the risk.

I charged in and bowled Viv four bouncers in a row. The umpire stepped in after the first three and Bruce Yardley quietly reminded me that I might be banned from the attack if I persisted.

I put the fifth ball into the block hole and, as I walked back to my mark, I deliberately indicated – so that Viv would see – to the bloke at square leg to drop back. My plan was that Viv would think he was going to cop aer bouncer, and he was quickly on the back foot in anticipation. But I fired him in a good length delivery that went between bat and pad to bowl him, without a single run on the scoreboard. In my excitement I ran down the wicket and gave the stumps a gentle kick. Suddenly there was hope!

I picked up David Ogilvie (9) to a spectacular catch by Mick Malone in the slips, which brought Greg Chappell in. I planned to bowl six to nine inches outside Greg's off-stump, but Rod instructed me to bowl a high delivery over his left shoulder, about 25 to 30cm above and to his left.

Everything went to plan. Rod was already in position when the Queensland captain, after making only two, gloved the delivery wide and high down leg side. If Rod hadn't known where the attempted hook would end up, he could not have covered enough ground and it would have been a boundary.

Mick got rid of Phil Carlson for one and when he added the other opener, Alan Jones (22), Queensland was 5–35. The WACA crowd was yelling, 'Kill, kill, kill!'

We kept our foot flat on the floor, and when I had Denis Schuller caught by Serjeant for a duck I had 4–21 off 7.3 overs. Queensland was out for 62 in the 21st over. Wayne Clark, 3–21, and Mick Malone, 2–19, were the only other two bowlers used, and they bowled magnificently.

I won the Man of the Match award, but when you look at our bowling performances and the brilliant catching and fielding that day, you'll see that it really was an amazing team effort to overcome such odds to win. It was a classic case of belief and execution combined, and I've no argument whatsoever with whoever dubbed it 'the Miracle Match'. ●

ROD SLATER

Around the water cooler

Lillee opened the bowling and wow, was he fired-up! The first delivery was wide, and Viv Richards couldn't get his bat to it, but the next three of four pounded the pitch just short of Viv and rose fiercely above the great West Indian's head. The umpire stopped Dennis and spoke directly in his ear, but it did nothing to deter Dennis and soon he had Viv out for a duck.

The next day, when we were back in the office (it was ridiculous, but yes, Dennis had to rock up to 'work' the next day), after congratulating Dennis on his magnificent performance, I asked what the umpire had said to him. 'He just asked me to watch his head,' said Dennis. 'And I said, "Sure, ump, but Viv better watch his head or I'll knock the fucking thing off!"'

Rod Slater, Dennis's old boss at Eurocars

This was a very proud moment. It was an honour to stand in as WA captain for the last few games of the season, culminating in WA winning the Sheffield Shield yet again. It was my last first-class game for WA as I retired from Test cricket after the last match of that season, Sydney v Pakistan.

The team that won the Sheffield Shield in my last game for Western Australia.

Captain Leftfield

I was fortunate enough to again play with Dennis for Western Australia in the early 1980s. Some memorable games were defined by his fierce determination and will to win. He was acting captain for several games in 1983–84, and his captaincy was sometimes out of left field. No game showed this more than a vital match against a very talented Victorian side. Dennis set the strangest field I have ever seen at the WACA to a Victorian batsman named Mick Taylor. Taylor had made four consecutive hundreds for Victoria and was strongly tipped to play for Australia in the following weeks.

With Tom Hogan bowling his left-arm orthodox, Dennis had a slip and a gully and two leg slips and a short fine square leg – so five fielders plus a keeper behind the wicket within a few metres of the bat, with a spinner bowling at the WACA. Tay-

lor was out for a duck on the fourth ball, caught Lillee, bowled Hogan at leg slip.

The Vics had us in trouble in the second innings; they were five wickets down needing only 70 more runs. They were cruising to a win when Dennis, once again, found his famous second wind and got us out of jail by taking five for about 20. His will to win rubbed off on those playing with him. Everyone around him just lifted a cog or two, and I'm sure some very great Australian cricketers would say the same.

One thing that I'm perhaps well placed to vouch for is what a genuine and grounded bloke Dennis is. So much has happened in the 50 years we've been friends, but I can honestly say that apart from getting balder and greyer (haven't we all?), Dennis hasn't changed a jot. He still gives 100 per cent to everything he does.

Wayne Hill, former cricketer for West Australia

FIGHTING FOR THE WACA

IF I KNEW THEN WHAT I KNOW NOW, THE development proposal for the WACA to become self-sufficient at its home ground would never have been started. Although I still think it was a terrific idea and was an excellent solution to the WACA's needs, I realise now that there was no way we were going to succeed – not with the obstacles that were in our way, and not with the number of our own people, never mind the external forces, that were starting to pull against us.

Early on, the new board had begun to turn the WACA around, setting in motion plans to repay its near-crippling debt and to revitalise its operations. But the infrastructure of the WACA Ground itself was antiquated and we needed to revamp it. My plan took shape once I met with Ascot Capital's David Van der Walt and Greg King, after an introduction by two great mates, Rod Duggan and Neil Earl.

In summary, the plan was to redevelop the WACA venue in stages. Some of the land would be utilised to build apartments, the income from which would be used to redevelop the ageing WACA infrastructure, eventually leading to a total redevelopment of the WACA Ground. Ascot Capital was amazing to work with all the way through, and I can't say enough about their commitment to the proposal. In July 2010 the plan received unanimous support from the WACA Board and over 90 per cent of

WACA members, and so work began on the incredibly time-consuming process of gaining planning permits for the proposal. Unfortunately the economic climate in Western Australia deteriorated during this time, so it was decided to put the development on hold until the economy improved. The opposing forces had by this time come increasingly into play.

David Van der Walt and Greg King were astonished and disappointed when, in 2014, the WACA decided to terminate their agreement with Ascot Capital, knowing that such a decision was to be at significant financial cost to the WACA. I was adamant that my negative vote in regard to this decision be recorded in the WACA Board meeting minutes. So much positive work had been done to get building approvals, and Ascot Capital was convinced that with patience awaiting the right market conditions, the original vision for the WACA Ground would be achieved. The decision to terminate the agreement, in my opinion, not only jeopardised the future of the WACA as a Test cricket venue, but it also squandered a considerable part of the cash reserves that we had fought so tenaciously to build.

The West Australian Government had decided to build a new stadium for football to replace the ageing Subiaco Oval. They pitched the billion-dollar Burswood project to the public as 'multipurpose', which meant it would be for activities other than football, including cricket.

Our proposed development at the WACA was clearly competition to their overall planned usage at Burswood, and possibly to other residential complexes planned external to WACA landholdings. We stated to the Government on numerous occasions that we would be happy to use Burswood for a few blockbusters, such as a 20/20 final, one-day final or an international one-dayer. This was on the proviso that the financial numbers stacked up – it would depend on cost versus crowd numbers etc. We emphasised that all Test cricket must remain at the home of cricket in WA.

In the Presidents Room during a Test match against England at the WACA in December 2013, I asked a very senior executive from Cricket Australia where he saw the future of Test cricket in WA. Much to my horror, he pointed to the game in

The stunningly beautiful setting that is the WACA Ground in Perth. Unlike most large iconic cricket grounds, which end up becoming concrete edifices, the WACA is more like English cricket stadia but has its own unique personality. That's what I and many people love about this ground. I feel it is slowly being abandoned and I am as sad as anyone to see its demise. To me it feels like an old Test jumper; it looks good, it's classy, it's got history and character, and you feel comfortable in it. Sure, it needs mending from time to time but you don't just throw it out.

progress. 'I want this,' he said, then pointed in the direction of Burswood, 'over there.'

You don't have to be Einstein to realise that we were in for a fight, which, with the cards stacked high against us, we couldn't win. More importantly, there were a few major opponents within the WACA hierarchy who had the same sentiment as that Cricket Australia Executive.

I stayed on as president for some time after these revelations to fight those machinations, but in the end I resigned in September of 2015 when our Board voted to sign a tripartite agreement with the Western Australia State Government and the WAFC (West Australian Football Commission, the state body of Aussie rules football, which has a very long lease on their current ground, Subiaco Oval). The agreement, in simple terms, meant that West Australian Football League (WAFL) football games would move to the WACA, clearing Subiaco Oval

the government to regain control over it. Supposedly, the government's part in the agreement was to contribute a large sum to develop the WACA Ground to a small crowd capacity so as to accommodate local football and cricket crowds along with staff from the WACA and WAFC.

We certainly had no problem sharing the WACA Ground with football, but I knew that this plan would, in fact, ensure that the WACA could never hold a major Test match or blockbuster again. The WACA Ground would in future only host what were then called 'third-tier' Test matches, along with international limited overs games, women's cricket, Sheffield Shield and domestic cricket (in other words, all games with smaller crowd attendance). Smaller crowds, smaller gate receipts. Same staff and maintenance costs.

My strongest reason against entering into such an agreement was that at that time the government had not definitely committed to contribute any money to this 'deal'. In today's political climate it would be a brave person who predicted that any substantive money would be forthcoming from this or any subsequent state government. And finally, to my current knowledge, the government has not yet stated the financial terms under which cricket matches will be played at Burswood, making the WACA Board's commitment to them even more remarkable. WA football stakeholders have been far more prudent and cautious in their negotiations.

I wouldn't agree to such a deal – or, rather, non-deal – and felt that neither should the WACA Board, and I said so. Unfortunately it fell on deaf ears as all the directors apart from me voted to sign this problematic document – remember it was supposed to be a tripartite agreement – when none of the other parties had agreed to sign (and, again to my knowledge at the time of writing, they still haven't done so). I walked out after the vote and tendered my resignation to the Board Chairman and WACA members shortly thereafter.

I made a short statement to the press: 'I cannot stand by and watch what is happening at the WACA. I do not wish to be part of it any longer.' Those who know me could read between the lines and understood my stance.

The WACA put forward that there were no problems between me, the WACA Board and the CEO, and created the impression that they were at a loss to understand why I pulled the pin.

I believe the originally stated billion-dollar cost for the new Perth Stadium will at least double by the time it is complete. By this, I am including the entire infrastructure necessary for each patron to attend the stadium and leave, with everything in between. I also believe that WA cricket cannot possibly keep the WACA and hire the new stadium as well as make the money necessary for grassroots cricket.

Imagine the sight of around 5000 people on day four of a Test match sitting in a 60,000 capacity stadium – and the viability of the cost to service that!

In spite of the stadium issue, I did enjoy my 11 years as president, meeting and working with some great people. I tried to make the Presidents Room a more informal, relaxed place to enjoy the cricket. Because, after all, *enjoying* the cricket is what it should all be about! ●

An unlikely administrator

As a limited opening batsman playing for North Perth in the WACA competition (in an era when the greats played club cricket if they did not have Test or state commitments) I encountered Dennis a few times in first grade matches. And, of course, most of them are unhappy memories.

But amid failures, I recall with pride surviving Dennis's opening spell in a club match only a week before his famous 8/29 against the Rest of the World at the WACA in 1971. Many years later, I casually remarked in company that he must have chosen not to waste any of his good stuff on me that day in advance of the bigger contests ahead. But Dennis insisted that he hated all batsmen equally and was always trying to see the back of them, no matter where he was playing.

It was a relief that one season Dennis was rehabilitating from back surgery, which meant we didn't have to face his bowling. But then he took to us with the bat, making an accomplished 70-odd against our club in a season where he scored the best part of 800 runs. He was equally determined with bat, ball and, as I'd discover later, at WACA Board level.

I had the pleasure of seeing most of Dennis's extraordinary achievements for Western Australia and Australia on the WACA turf, but it was behind the scenes that I got to know him. I was surprised, in 2004, when a group of people persuaded Dennis to stand for president in the 2004 WACA member elections for board positions. I wasn't surprised by his commitment to WA cricket, rather that '*the* Dennis Lillee', so famous for his stoushes with

the cricket establishment, would agree to become an honorary administrator.

By this time I was nearly two decades though my administration career with the WACA in a variety of roles including membership manager, association secretary and several extended stints as acting chief executive. The WACA had fallen on hard times since the turn of the 21st century – after an era of playing success, ground redevelopment and the WACA being Perth's premier multi-sport venue the organisation was desperately in need of positive change.

Dennis won office in a landslide, leading a new wave of board members that included fellow former Test representatives Graeme Wood and Sam Gannon and the enormously talented, soon-to-be WACA Board Chairman, David Williams. They inherited a dire financial situation, with the WACA almost $15 million in debt and with income diminishing. The Association's reputation and credibility with its major stakeholders – WACA members, the wider cricket family, sponsors, media, and government – was rock bottom. Urgent action and strong leadership were critical for its survival.

David Williams was the energy and intellectual catalyst for change, while Dennis was the inspiration and conduit to the 'doors of power'. A previously unsympathetic State Government quickly stumped up $5 million to help the WACA through its immediate cash crisis. Tough decisions were made to streamline the business, with David and Dennis at the helm.

I could tell almost immediately that Dennis had left his comfort zone to join the WACA administration. He didn't enjoy any trivia at board meetings, and engaged only when important issues arose. He spoke rarely but when he did it was incisive on a surprisingly diverse range of issues, far from limited to cricket matters. Despite the uneasy fit, such was Dennis's love for cricket and commitment to the WACA that he served for six two-year terms – unsurprisingly never contested come election time.

The duo of David Williams and Dennis, aided by CEO Tony Dodemaide and Graeme Wood, enabled the WACA's former debt to be repaid and replaced by similar-sized cash reserves in the first seven years of Dennis's presidency. The WACA's reputation with cricket's stakeholders also improved immeasurably. They appreciated being heard and involved in key strategic decisions.

Having been a substantial influence in reversing the short-term future prospects of the WACA, Dennis was also concerned for the long-term future of the ground itself. One of his many worldwide contacts – international property developers and cricket lovers Ascot Capital – potentially held a key to that issue.

The two parties entered negotiations, and an agreement was reached (with near unanimous approval of voting WACA members) whereby Ascot Capital would initially provide the WACA with a $9m interest-free loan to ease its cash flow concerns, and when market conditions were most favourable (in conjunction with the WACA) residential and commercial units would be constructed under strata title on those parts of WACA land not necessary for the conduct of its core business.

The first $105 million of profits from those projects was to be returned to the WACA for ground improvements that the WACA deemed to be appropriate. Profits beyond $105 million were to be shared between WACA and Ascot on a 70 per cent to 30 per cent basis in favour of the WACA.

I and many others, including respected professionals in the property industry, believed it was a great deal for the WACA and, in my opinion, represented the best chance to not only preserve the heritage of the WACA Ground but also to ensure its long-term future as the home of cricket in Western Australia. If property prices in Perth had held up to the levels expected during the planning phase of this project, the Ascot deal would have been an outstanding result.

Many years were needed to obtain planning approvals, formulate designs and await the best market climate for the project to commence. When the project did not proceed, perceptions were created that it was a poor deal for the WACA and somehow that Dennis Lillee, who had given so many years to cricket in WA, was responsible for the subsequent liability that the WACA incurred when the board chose to abandon the agreement with Ascot Capital near the end of Dennis's time as president. Those perceptions are unfair.

It is no secret that for many years some WACA Board members did not view it as critical that the WACA Ground stage all first-class cricket in Perth and were keen to explore the possibility of the highest profile cricket matches being played at Subiaco Oval or any other headquarters that may have been provided for AFL football in Perth.

Certainly the West Australia Government were anxious to see as much product as possible for their new state-funded stadium, and Cricket Australia, who had long questioned the merits of state association-owned grounds, were also keen for high-profile cricket to be played at the new venue.

In the end, the board of the time convinced themselves that rather than considering the future profitability of the redevelopment, it would abandon the Ascot Capital agreement, incur an immediate and substantial financial liability and enter into an agreement with the State Government to play high-profile Test and other popular cricket matches on yet-to-be-established terms at the new Perth Stadium at Burswood. The board could have continued to assess the viability of the redevelopment project without time limitations, which was a surprisingly generous offer from Ascot, given that they would financially benefit immediately at the cessation of the agreement. Those sitting in judgement of Dennis or Ascot and the abandoned agreement often overlook the benefits of the $9 million interest-free loan made to the WACA in their time of great need, and the general terms of the profit distribution in redevelopment, which favoured the WACA.

They also ignore that previous WACA boards under David and Dennis had frequently stated that they were open to certain high-profile cricket matches being played at a new government-funded stadium, if the terms for such staging were in the best interests of the WACA and other cricket stakeholders. Strategically, those boards believed that having the alternative of a redeveloped WACA Ground, or at least part thereof, would strengthen the WACA's negotiating position in such discussions and provide the best chance of the WACA remaining the home of Test match cricket in Perth, as WACA forefa-

thers and the public had worked so hard for in the past.

As association secretary at the WACA for all but the last eighteen months of Dennis's presidency, I was able to see close-up his fierce determination to become the best and most effective president he could be, even if he never grew to relish the role. Indeed, I remember before one AGM of members, Dennis told me he'd rather face Joel Garner and Malcolm Marshall in their prime than chair such a meeting. But he never shirked the courage of his convictions and always stood up for what he believed was right, even if it was to the detriment of his own standing in some quarters. Dennis's high profile made him an enormously effective representative and advocate for the WACA, but regretfully it also made him a convenient scapegoat when one was needed.

In 2015, more than a year after I had retired as secretary, Dennis walked away from the WACA – in a manner that was uncharacteristically very quiet and without warning. He confided in me privately that 12 years of administration and boardroom intrigue had worn him down. Dennis was the last of the 2004 'new wave' board to retire, having gallantly outstayed Graeme Wood, David Williams and Sam Gannon. I hope that a new generation will step up and fight to keep the WACA as the home of cricket in Western Australia just as Dennis and the others had done so valiantly.

I was privileged to work closely with Dennis and have developed a warm friendship with him and his wife, Helen, a woman of great patience, intellect and wisdom who has been a vital part of Dennis's life for half a century.

Geoff Havercroft, former secretary of the WACA

An effective partnership

Unlike many of the contributors to this book, my relationship with Dennis was formed off the field. It was 2004, the beginning of his tenure as President of the WACA, and I was privileged to work in harness with Dennis for nine of those years as Chairman of the WACA. The WACA has always had a dual system of president and chairman. For us it was a splendid partnership.

When we were elected in 2004 the WACA's off-field position was dire, as has been explained elsewhere. Shortly into the rescue mission, the board resolved to carry out a total review of the organisation. The review committee conducted over fifty interviews with a huge range of stakeholders including groundsmen, players, board members, sponsors, administrative staff and WACA members. Dennis did not miss an interview!

After the report was finalised and accepted by the board there was a dreadful day when many cuts were made to the employment ranks. Dennis managed to reopen the doors to the State Government and, based on the revitalised board and economic plan, the Labor Government of Gallop and then Carpenter gave the WACA a $5 million loan/grant payment over several years. This payment, coupled with many wise decisions by the board

and management, and aided by two outstanding CEOs in Tony Dodemaide and Graeme Wood, enabled us to record nine successive years of profit and at the end of the 2012–13 financial year we could point to approx $13 million in funds and no debt.

It was a lot of hard work. We made money wherever we could, like developing the Lillee Club, which was masterfully run by vice president Sam Gannon for many years and contributed a significant sum to the bottom line. Dennis is not only a man of action but also of ideas. His contribution to the Packer revolution is for other pages but his thinking should never be underestimated.

The WACA Ground is the only ground in Australia owned by the state cricket body and has been since the 1890s. That presented a unique opportunity for a visionary plan to develop part of the freehold as an accommodation precinct. Through Dennis's contacts the WACA entered into a partnership with a group of wealthy but altruistic South African businessmen who had immigrated to Australia.

The agreement, which was made available to WACA members to peruse, provided for the WACA to receive the first $100 million notwithstanding that the JV partners contributed nearly $3 million in risk money to achieve the necessary approvals. Not surprisingly the members approved the plan overwhelmingly. It would require a book – not just a few pages – to fully explain this saga, which should have been one of the great sporting projects.

The WACA was in serious need of attention. The standards for members and the public were unacceptable. No one felt that more keenly than Dennis, but he also knew the big picture was what had to be painted. No stadium in Australia has been built or refurbished without government money, yet here was an opportunity for a government to work in partnership with a sporting body that started with an offer of $100 million over the life of the three-stage development. The obtaining of the various approvals, albeit with some negative requirements, saw a revaluation from under $3 million to over $45 million of the land.

The timing of this WACA project coincided with the development of the Burswood stadium, and it is a tragedy that many people in government and in the WACA were unable to see that both projects were possible and that we could have had two world-class stadiums, of varying sizes. The hard facts are that Test matches rarely (only on two days in my nine-year tenure) filled the house. We lamented on many occasions that we no longer had Graeme Wood at the helm or that we were not still dealing with a sympathetic government.

Now we have a situation where the Test matches involving India, South Africa and England will no longer be held on a pitch that Peter Lalor marvellously described as '22 yards of pure evil', and where the crowds bayed at the southern end, 'Lillee, Lillee, Lillee.'

Call Dennis and me optimists, but we think that despite the efforts of some in cricket administration, the government and its minions, the fat lady has not yet sung over the WACA. The JV partners hold residual rights and the marvellous location of the WACA has not moved. This irreplaceable cricket ground, one of the greatest and best known in the world, awaits only an administration and government with vision and courage to take advantage when the property market recovers.

David Williams, former chairman of the WACA

I loved the opportunity to race in a few Celebrity Challenges once cricket finished.

12

AWAY FROM CRICKET

Away from cricket family is my main focus. Helen and I love being grandparents, and having all our extended family nearby. Apart from that, I've developed a taste for wine in my later years and have always loved fishing.

REDS AND REELS

DURING MY PLAYING CAREER, GOING DOWN TO the pub and sinking a few beers with my mates wasn't really my style. I didn't even like the taste of beer; besides, there were more productive things to do, like pounding the pavement and having a bowl in the nets.

That was my attitude and general approach to drinking throughout my career, yet there were others who wanted to portray me in a completely different light. In the television production called *Howzat*, which set out to give an insight into the establishing and running of World Series Cricket, I saw someone I didn't recognise. Here was this fast bowler named Dennis Lillee, who Kerry Packer had signed up, sitting in the dressing room after a day's play draining a can of beer.

I admit to drinking plenty of water and so I copped a bit of a ribbing over the beer scene when *Howzat* went to air. Another member of our team, Doug Walters, also fell victim to the vivid imagination of the producer when the actor playing him was seen smoking a cigarette in the nets. Nobody liked a ciggie and a game of cards more than Douggie, but there is no way he would ever light up at practice.

After I retired, apart from the occasional rum, I never drank much beyond a few beers when out for dinner or catching up with old mates at the pub. That all changed after Helen and I were invited to attend McLaren Vale's Bushing Festival in South Australia. It was just a little holiday, and I don't think I even did any wine-tasting.

When it came time to head home, a policeman who had organised our trip (and who happened to have the same name as champion West Australian fast bowler Laurie Mayne) offered to give us a lift to the airport. Along the way, Laurie kept stopping at vineyards, and each time he did he'd place a case of wine in the boot of the car. We assumed, unkindly, that this copper was on the take!

Collecting our suitcases at Perth airport, an airport official reminded us to collect our excess baggage. We didn't know what he was talking about but turned a corner to find all of the wine our policeman/chauffeur had picked up along the way.

We were living in a little weatherboard house without air conditioning at the time, and had nothing in the way of storage space, so all the wine was stored under the bed and in every nook and cranny we could find. The boxes remained there for years, and the wine was mostly 8–10 years old when we finally decided to 'have a taste'. Well, that was like a Eureka moment for me, and I've since become something of an aficionado!

I've got an ample cellar these days, which is catalogued and features many of our favourite wines. I suppose it's a good illustration of how times have changed, that my cricket memorabilia is stuffed into

These are the kind of tours I most enjoy these days, and they're so much the better because Helen and I can do them together. This was an introduction to French wines at Chateauneuf du Pape in the south-east of France. We enjoy French wine but still prefer to drink Australian. Between sips, Helen was behind the camera.

boxes in the shed, while the cellar looks pristine. Our tastes take in some French and Italian wines these days but, in my opinion, Australian winemakers still produce some of the best in the world.

My other passion in life is, was and always will be, fishing.

I remember my late brother, Trevor, and I riding our bikes about 10 kilometres to the Garratt Road Bridge where we would try our luck catching garfish. As I grew older I fully intended to spend a lot of my spare time wetting a line, but cricket invariably got in the way.

While most cricketers head for the golf course when they have some spare time on tour, I usually found someone to take me fishing. I have especially happy memories of casting a line in the West Indies and New Zealand.

While fishing near Gracetown in the southwest of WA, a wonderful lady named Beryl Ryan taught me the art of catching herring with a flick rod. This method, though, is limited to rock fishing, so now I use a rod and reel and rarely go home empty-handed.

One of the best feelings I get these days is not pushing off on a run to bowl, but pushing my dinghy off a sandbank and into the river in the south of Western Australia. Even if I don't catch anything, I always find the outing most therapeutic. But it's that little bit more special when I return with some yellowfin tuna or King George whiting, herring or flounder, not to mention a few blue swimmer crabs. And I'll have a nice wine to accompany it. ●

Most of my teammates liked golf (or drinking) during down times, but I occasionally got them out fishing. A bunch of us, including Thommo, Rod Marsh and Kim Hughes, had a great day fishing on a boat in New Zealand between Tests on the 1981–82 tour. The lads weren't too impressed with the puny shark I caught (top left).

I've always loved fishing and it's still one of my absolute favourite things in life. Even if I don't catch anything, engaging with nature really helps clear my head.

LEFT: Quite proud of this trout caught at London Lakes, Tasmania.

ABOVE: A couple of nice dolphin fish caught offshore from Perth and Rottnest Island.

BELOW: Fishing near Darwin in the Northern Territory with Adam, our eldest son – a stunning mackerel.

Fishing lessons with Aunty Beryl

Neil and I met DK though my aunty, Beryl Ryan. Dennis had recently bought a new, you-beaut fishing rod and reel worth about $350 and was keen to try it out around Gracetown. He went up to north point to try out the new gear and found himself fishing alongside Aunty Beryl, who was fishing with a $20 bamboo pole with a line and two hooks attached (we called it a flick rod).

After half an hour, Beryl's bucket was filling up, while DK's was still hollow. Beryl suggested that Dennis try the flick rod, but he just laughed. Another half-hour later, Beryl's bucket was full and DK, for the umpteenth time, was trying to untangle the new line and his expensive gear. Beryl took pity on him and put a dozen herring in his bucket. DK was a bit embarrassed, but he didn't give the fish back. They became great friends over time.

DK asked Beryl if she knew anyone who could take him shooting, and that's when Neil and I came into the picture. DK was as good at shooting as he was at fishing. He sprayed the paddocks trying to shoot a rabbit; every now and then the rabbit would look up to see what the noise was and continue grazing. They knew they were safe.

DK was already a champion cricketer when we met. He knew Neil and I played cricket for the Hawks Cricket Club at Margaret River and asked us if he could do some net practise on a regular basis so he could get fit for the coming season. Neil and I were playing footy at the time so we were pretty fit, but when it came to cricket our training was once a week and consisted of one lap around the oval in the car, 20 minutes of nets, two hours of solid drinking, then home. DK's training was a little different.

We went to the nets in Busselton for the first session, with Neil mainly as a bowler and me apparently as the batsman. On arrival, I went straight to the nets and started putting the pads on, but DK said we had to warm up first. After 10 laps of the oval and 20 minutes of stretching we were finally ready. DK was bowling off the short run. After about 20 minutes he asked me if I was feeling comfortable, and explained how he was just trying to get his rhythm. Foolishly, I told him that I had to have a cup of tea and a bun while waiting for the ball to arrive. Well, his smile disappeared, and soon mine did too.

DK turned around, placed his marker 10 metres further back, grabbed a new ball, and leaned into his run. I felt very lonely when I saw him charging in with my helmet as his target. I heard the ball whistle past, about two inches above my helmet, and crash into the back of the net. The next half-dozen balls landed in DK's half, and I could offer no resistance. I could hear Neil in the background, 'You were saying something, Rod?' DK knew what he was doing and I wasn't going to get hurt, but I got the message loud and clear. Finally, the lesson was finished. I was keen for a beer, but DK said we had to warm down. That could mean another five laps around the oval, 20 minutes of stretching and, for DK, a 12 kilometre run!

Much safer (for us) is his passion for wine. He's got a large cellar and counts every bottle in and out like the bank teller

Not a bad catch on a four-wheel drive trip to the north-west of Perth.

he used to be. Whenever we're allowed in, he watches us like a hawk. He always brings two or three bottles of beautiful red when we go out for dinner – it's as certain as someone coming up to meet him and shake his hand or get a photograph. He always handles these exchanges warmly.

You can't blame people for wanting to meet DK after he gave them so much to enjoy. But sometimes people could pick their moments better. My wife, Debbie,

and I went to Europe with DK and Helen recently. We were walking the Cinque Terre trail through the mountains of Italy, a curious choice given that it turns out DK is terrified of heights. He was literally hugging the edges as we walked along, when out of the blue came, 'You're Dennis Lillee, aren't you? Look everyone – it's DK Lillee!' I think that might have been one time he wished he wasn't!

Rod Duggan and Neil Earl, friends

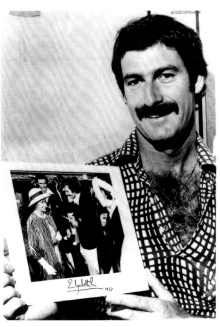

I've always felt the link to England closely through my grandparents and I'm happy to be considered a monarchist. At the top is the first time I met Prince Philip. At the Centenary Test in Australia, I cheekily asked the Queen for her autograph. She demurred, implying that if she signed for me, she'd have to sign for everyone in the MCG. I was overjoyed when later I received a print of our encounter signed by HRH (centre right)! Centre left was the next time we met. Nobody expects awards of recognition like an Order of Australia, but it's good to be appreciated for your contributions. In this case, it was more about my involvement in charities and not-for-profit organisations. I was previously awarded an MBE for my cricket efforts.

SIR ROBERT MENZIES

95 COLLINS STREET MELBOURNE VICTORIA 3000 TELEPHONE 63 9463

22nd November, 1974

My dear Denis Lillee

I am ashamed that I have not written to you since our meeting at the M.C.G. to tell you how much I enjoyed reading your book.

I was very proud to be chosen as the recipient of one of the first copies before release, and appreciated your courtesy in meeting me on my arrival at the ground. I watched the match with great interest and will be following your fortunes when the Test Matches begin. Good luck to both of you.

With warmest regards,

Yours sincerely,

(R.G. MENZIES)

Messrs. D. Lillee &
Ian Brayshaw.
- - -

PREMIER OF WESTERN AUSTRALIA
PERTH
WESTERN AUSTRALIA 6000

4th March, 1977

Dear Dennis,

Congratulations on yet another fine performance.

You certainly finished off the New Zealand tour in grand style.

Also, thanks again for the part you, Rod Marsh, and others played in making sure we had a successful Sheffield Shield season with the Shield remaining in Western Australia.

I notice there has been a little bit of paper comment regarding yourself.

Do not let this worry you. Perhaps I should say "Welcome to the Club"!

It seems to be inevitable that when one achieves success there are always people ready to move in and express their thoughts in their own extraordinary ways.

Perhaps the best way to deal with situations like this is to ignore them and feel sorry for the people who are so frustrated in their own endeavours that they have to resort to criticism of others.

Kindest regards to you and your family, and every good wish for both the match to be played in Perth later this week and also for the Centenary Test to be played against M.C.C.

The latter is certainly a history-making match and one which I am sure will bring a lot of satisfaction to you and your colleagues.

Please pass on my best wishes to Rod Marsh and the other boys in the team.

Yours sincerely,

PREMIER

MR. D.K. LILLEE,

Here's some of the precious correspondence I've received down the years from our most senior politicians congratulating me on achievements. Meeting with legendary Australian prime ministers like Robert Menzies (here with my mate Ian Brayshaw giving him an advance copy of our book) and Bob Hawke (at a golf day) was special, while having a statue in my honour outside the MCG is just extraordinary. Fortunately, as is the case here, I've always had mates to keep me well and truly grounded.

No mute button

Like most Aussie backyards, ours was constantly alive with intense cricket matches. As the youngest of four kids, I needed aggression to stay alive in the contest. I enjoyed mimicking the graceful Terry Alderman, his smooth gentle run-up and subtle outswing to a packed slips cordon. But when that wasn't cutting it, I turned my attention to the firebrand that was DK Lillee. That's who I wanted to be! Powerful, aggressive, athletic, mentally strong, hardworking and charismatic.

Once I realised I was none of the above, I made my third positional change and focused on being like DK's partner, Rodney Marsh. Let the fast bowlers do all the hard work! Just squat down behind the stumps to accept (or drop) the many edges they induce from nervous batsmen. What a combo: caught Marsh, bowled Lillee! I decided I wanted to be the 'Marsh'.

Little did I realise it would actually happen, playing in a Chairman's XI match at Lilac Hill against Pakistan in October 1995: 'Saleem Elahi, caught Gilly, bowled Lillee 0.'

I could have retired that day a very content young cricketer. Luckily I didn't, but I got to know Dennis better from then. I'd met him a few times prior, mainly at the Cricket Academy. He and Rod Marsh were brilliant in teaching the next generation about the big picture, not just technique and skills – like how to balance life as a professional cricketer, and when to have fun and switch off from the stress and pressure. And geez, didn't they know how to do that well!

Their message was based on good old-fashioned values: work hard, play hard and then enjoy a break before cranking up again. All this is only possible if you can look in the mirror and honestly tell the person staring back at you that you are keeping it all balanced.

I've always felt a positive vibe around Dennis – the upbeat tempo of someone that is always looking to improve but have fun along the way. The era I played in idolised those guys from the 1970s and 80s, often referencing their characters and achievements for motivation. My heart skips a beat even now when my phone rings and his name appears as the caller. A true legend.

My only doubts about Dennis are around his understanding of modern technology. We were filming a television commercial some years ago, and Dennis and I were sitting on one side of the WACA Ground with roving microphones on. The whole production team and cameraman were positioned all the way across the other side.

In between takes, Dennis let off some steam about a particular director's assistant. Out of the corner of my eye, I noticed a commotion on the far side of the ground. The sound technician was jumping up and down, waving his arms around and banging his ears. It eventually dawned on us that Dennis hadn't turned his mike off, and the entire crew was tuned into every word Dennis and I were saying.

We continued the shoot, with Dennis unfazed – as always, saying exactly what he felt, and never backing down.

Adam Gilchrist, 96 Tests for Australia

"IT'S NEVER TOO EARLY TO START SAVING FOR CHRISTMAS."

JOIN THE [BUILDING SOCIETY] CHRISTMAS CLUB NOW.

Howzat?

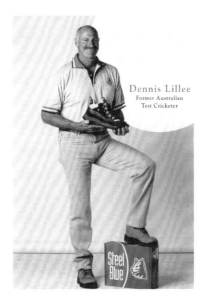

Dennis Lillee
Former Australian
Test Cricketer

Steel Blue

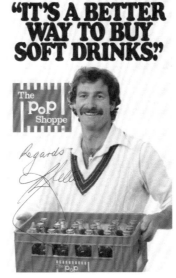

"IT'S A BETTER WAY TO BUY SOFT DRINKS"

The Pop Shoppe

Regards

"HOW MILK USED TO BE – BUT CHOLESTEROL FREE"

Brownes
No Cholesterol
Dairy Wise

I've been honoured to be associated with many terrific brands and people over the years, but my involvement with Steel Blue Boots probably tops the lot. It's a great company with great people who have become great friends.

Just the tonic

My relationship with Dennis started when he was no longer bowling – well, not at anywhere near 150kph – and I was no longer good enough to even make the local thirds.

My family and I were about a decade into establishing our national retail pharmacy chain, Chemist Warehouse, and, as a rusted-on cricket tragic, I was always keen to use cricketers in our advertising. If you're going to use a cricketer to promote your brand, align your brand with a legend; if you are going to use a legend … use Dennis! So it came to pass around 2012 that Dennis became 'our opener'. The campaign with Dennis was a huge commercial success, but even better was the positive experience of getting to know the man himself.

I came to realise that Dennis is not just a legend of the game; he is a legend of a man. My eldest son, Lachlan, is as cricket-mad as me, but fortunately he's more talented. When he was only nine, his determination to train harder than anyone else to become the best bowler saw his little body break down. He was diagnosed with a repetitive strain injury in his lower back and instructed not to bowl for at least three months (in other words, the entire cricket season). He was devastated, inconsolable and distraught. Three months for a nine-year-old may as well be a lifetime, and my wife and I couldn't comfort him. So I rang Dennis and asked if he had any advice I could pass on.

But Dennis didn't want to talk to me. He asked to speak to Lachy. Over the course of ten minutes, I could hear Dennis talking and see Lachy's face brightening. He explained to Lachy the whole story of his own back issues, the long road to recovery, and how he came through it. Dennis promised Lachy he'd give him bowling lessons to correct his action and to minimise risk of future injury. Then he apologised and said he had to go, because the media were waiting for him to present a Young Cricketer of the Year award.

Not only had Dennis taken the time, while being pressed by the media and cricket officialdom, to talk to Lachy, he had promised to coach him once his back was better. As a man of his word, that is precisely what he did. The measure of the man is not gauged by his capacity to dismiss a batsman standing 22 yards away, but by his capacity to be selfless, compassionate, caring and kind. Dennis Lillee stacks up.

Damien Gance, founder and director of Chemist Warehouse

The scarecrow

Dennis has always had a great sense of humour, and there's one story that exemplifies his humour and perseverance in everything he does.

Every Easter for years after we all stopped playing cricket, Dennis and Helen had a group of us down to their property about 400 kilometres south of Perth. It is particularly remote because Dennis always craved privacy, and you have to travel along many secluded and unsealed roads to get there. Visitors have recorded many near misses, so Dennis would always forewarn us if he had encountered many kangaroos on the way in. He said there'd been a lot lately and to drive slowly, and I thought nothing of it when Dennis asked me to call him when we turned off the main highway – if we got into trouble, he would know roughly where we were. How considerate of him!

I dutifully called him from a neighbour's house when I turned onto the unsealed road (we had no mobile coverage). There was no moon, and thick fog and drizzle made visibility very difficult. It made the drive in more eerie than usual. (Typical arsy Dennis, just the sort of night he wanted.) We'd been driving for about 30 minutes or so, with the lights on high beam and my wife, Lorraine, and I on high alert. Lorraine noticed something on the road, just in the limit of the high beam; we figured it must have been a dead kangaroo.

We continued driving slowly towards the scene and realised it was too big for a kangaroo. *Maybe it's a cow*, I was thinking, when, to my horror, I noticed a vehicle on the side of the road with its driver's door open. *It must be a body on the road*! Then

we noticed that the body was covered in blood! We panicked, figuring we'd stumbled across an ambush or a murder, and just wanted to get the hell out of there.

Out of the darkness, I saw some figures running towards us and I planted my foot on the accelerator. Just as I drew level with the 'body' I heard someone laughing. I immediately recognised the very distinctive laugh of one of our long-time mates. And then the two other 'murderers' came out of the darkness. They were nearly wetting themselves with laughter at how they'd scared the crap out of us.

In their elaborate plan, they'd got the ute from the house, drove it just off the road and left the driver's door open. Then they got a scarecrow from a neighbour, covered it with tomato sauce and laid it out in the middle of the road. Dennis had planned the prank for weeks; I don't know when or why, but, typically, once he had the idea he followed through. Unlike storys about his cricketing exploits, he likes to embellish this tale more and more every year.

I have vowed to seek revenge and have tried several times, but he's always been one step ahead of me. He knows it's coming, though, and I like to think that the years I've caused him nervous looks over his shoulder will make the payback that much sweeter.

Bruce Laird, 21 Tests for Australia

Singalong with Dennis (and Cyndi Lauper)

Even before I knew Dennis, he was in- volved in my wedding. My late brother and best man, Des, decided to calm my nerves on my wedding day by taking me to a hotel close to the church. Western Australia were playing Queensland in what later became known as 'the Miracle Match', and we got so immersed in Dennis's brilliant bowling that I almost missed my own wedding! I just made it, and married my childhood sweetheart, Jan. Now, nearly 40 years on, we're proud parents of six great children, and our beautiful granddaughter was born in 2016.

Dennis was one of my sporting idols. I greatly admired his amazing passion and competitive character. The first time I met him was in 1983, when we literally bumped into each other in a restaurant in Sydney. I invited him to join me and Cyndi Lauper, who was on a promo tour, and we established an immediate rapport.

After dinner I took Cyndi and DK to the Sebel Townhouse. On the way we all sang 'Girls Just Want to Have Fun' at the top of our voices, standing up through the sunroof. DK called Rod Marsh, who couldn't believe he was talking to Cyndi Lauper. A great night ended only when the sun came up.

We've shared many great times at our house, including plenty of backyard cricket sessions with both our families, who get along fabulously. One weekend in the 1990s, Dennis brought fish over to cook for lunch. Jan said she would take care of it and Dennis and I ducked out for a drink, telling Jan we'd be back in an hour. Heavy rain washed out the local sporting fixtures and it seemed most of the Northern

Districts cricketers ended up at the pub. They couldn't believe their eyes – DK at their local! He was so generous with them, and they were mesmerised by his humour, passion and presence. We returned home, fairly sheepishly, at about 8pm that night.

DK really has a gift for connecting with everyone, from airport baggage handlers, to people at the pub, right through to prime ministers. He has a big heart and has made a huge contribution to youth development programs and charities.

When we established the Sony Foundation Australia in 1999, Dennis was the first person I called to join as a board director. He said yes in a heartbeat, and he made an incredible contribution to the Sony Foundation as a board member

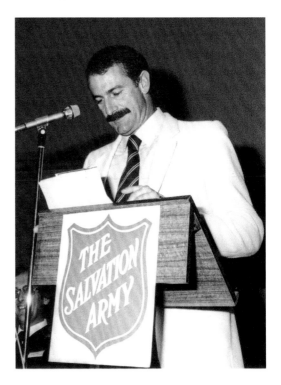

up until 2012, and as a life member ever since. He has supported all of the Foundation's programs, such as the holiday respite camps for special needs children, the 'You Can' youth cancer centres, and fundraising events. The Foundation has raised and distributed over $22 million for youth-related causes. The Foundation also partnered with him on the Dennis Lillee Disabled Sports Foundation, which provided activity days hosted by local schools, with special equipment for children with severe disabilities.

In 1998, I went through a bit of adversity in my career after trying to do too much and burning the candle at both ends. Dennis was straight on the phone and flew over from Perth to support me personally. As someone who'd been through tough times himself, he was able to give me amazing insight and advice that I will never forget. I am now in my 46th year with Sony Music, their longest-serving employee globally.

Dennis has always been in my corner. We will forever be loyal friends. He is a man's man with a wonderful, generous character. I have enormous respect for him, and I cherish our friendship. As my late mother used to say, 'True friends are like diamonds, precious and rare; false friends are like autumn leaves, found everywhere.' Dennis will always be a shining diamond and I love him to bits.

Denis Handlin AM, CEO and chairman of Sony Music Entertainment (Australia and New Zealand)

ABOVE: I was at a Sony Music function with Tina Arena and Denis Handlin. What a great singer! (Tina, that is...)

OPPOSITE: I've always thought that if I'm going to do something without getting paid, then it should be for charity or a mate. I've been delighted to lend my support to many charities over the years – but I'm pretty sure I got as much from them in experiences, which have helped me keep perspective, as they've ever got from me.

SIMPLY RED

Hello Dennis best wishes from Mick

My happy snaps with celebrities.

CLOCKWISE FROM TOP LEFT: An autograph from Mick Hucknall, who is a Lancashire Cricket fan and member; with football royalty, Dermott Brereton; with Rod Marsh and the legendary Bert Newton; John Farnham 'ripping the piss' out of my tie featuring the seven dwarfs; cricket-mad Michael Parkinson, with whom I've remained good friends; the band Chicago, who knew nothing about cricket but had us on stage trying to sing 'C'mon Aussie, C'mon'; enjoying a Bundy Rum with Paul Kelly; and finally, the great Elton John, who also loves cricket and has regularly invited myself and my former teammates to his performances over the years.

ABOVE: Backyard cricket with family is the same across the country, although I remember the last time we tried to play there wasn't a single bat in the house and I had to nail two bits of wood together so my grandkids could play. I know, it's unAustralian!

RIGHT: Our granddaughters Ajahna, Stella and India, who bring so much extra joy to our lives.

RIGHT: 'Dennis is an extraordinary man, as many contributors to this book can attest. He has enriched my life since we were teenagers and we have had so much fun!'

Helen, Mrs DK

Grandfather duties take up much of my spare time these days, and I couldn't be happier – apart from early on Christmas morning. Actually, early any morning can be hard work for me.

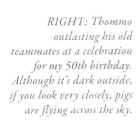

LEFT: With our youngest son, Dean, in the Pilbara.

RIGHT: Thommo outlasting his old teammates at a celebration for my 50th birthday. Although it's dark outside, if you look very closely, pigs are flying across the sky.

TEST HIGHLIGHTS

Made his debut at the age of 21 years 195 days and recorded the first of his 355 wickets when he dismissed JH Edrich on the first day. Added the wickets of APE Knott, R Illingworth, JA Snow and RGD Willis to return figures of 28.3-0-84-5 in his first innings (v England at Adelaide Oval, 1971)

Scored an undefeated 73 off 103 balls, hitting three sixes and eight fours in recording what remained his highest score in all first-class cricket (v England at Lord's, London, 1975)

Overtook R Benaud's Australian record of 248 wickets in 63 Tests and became the sixth bowler to take 250 (v India at the MCG, 1981)

Career-best figures of 8/29 (off 7.1 overs) came at the WACA against a star-studded Rest of the World team that toured Australia in 1971–72 in place of the banned South African team, although these were not officially counted as Test matches.

Took his 100th wicket when he achieved the first of his nine dismissals of IVA Richards at this level (v West Indies at Woolloongabba, Brisbane, 1975)

Took the wicket of HA Gomes and surpassed the world Test record of 309 wickets held by LR Gibbs for almost six years (v West Indies at the MCG, 1981)

Extended his world Test record to 355, 95 of them caught by RW Marsh to establish an unbeaten record for any bowler/wicketkeeper combination in Test cricket.

Retired from international cricket at the age of 34 years, 172 days (v Pakistan at the SCG, 1984)

WORLD SERIES SUPERTESTS
BOWLING AND FIELDING SUMMARY

SEASON	VENUE	MATCHES	OVERS	MDNS	RUNS	WKTS	AVGE	BEST	5WI	10WM	CT
1977-78	A	5	152.4	11	765	21	36.42	5-82	1	-	2
1978-79	NZ	1	32	11	89	12	7.41	7-59	2	1	-
1978-79	A	4	189.3	68	382	23	16.60	7-23	2	-	-
1978-79	WI	5	178.4	27	653	23	28.39	6-125	1	-	4
TOTALS		15	552.5	117	1889	79	23.91	7-23	6	1	6

TEST RECORD

SEASON	MATCH	VENUE	BATTING		BOWLING			
			NO	RUNS	OVERS	MAIDENS	RUNS	WICKETS
1970-71	1 ENGLAND 6	ADELAIDE	10	10	28.3	-	84	5
			-		7	-	40	-
	2 ENGLAND 7	SYDNEY	10	6	13	5	32	1
			10	0	14	-	43	2
1972	3 ENGLAND 1	MANCHESTER	11	1	29	14	40	2
			11	0	30	8	66	6
	4 ENGLAND 2	LORD'S	11	2	28	3	90	2
			-		21	6	50	2
	5 ENGLAND 3	NOTTINGHAM	11	0	29	15	35	4
			-		25	10	40	2
	6 ENGLAND 4	LEEDS	11	0	26.1	10	39	2
			10	7	5	2	7	1
	7 ENGLAND 5	THE OVAL	11	0	24.2	7	58	5
			-		32.2	8	123	5
1972-73	8 PAKISTAN 1	ADELAIDE	10	14	20.3	7	49	4
			-		15	3	53	1
	9 PAKISTAN 2	MELBOURNE	-		16.6	1	90	1
			11	2	11	1	59	1
	10 PAKISTAN 3	SYDNEY	10	2	10	2	34	1
			11	0	23	5	68	3
1972-73	11 WEST INDIES 1	KINGSTON	-		26	4	112	-
			-		6	1	20	-
1974-75	12 ENGLAND 1	BRISBANE	9	15	23	6	73	2
			-		12	2	25	2
	13 ENGLAND 2	PERTH	9	11	16	4	48	2
			-		22	5	59	2
	14 ENGLAND 3	MELBOURNE	9	2	20	2	70	2
			9	14	17	3	55	2
	15 ENGLAND 4	SYDNEY	9	8	19.1	2	66	2
			-		21	5	65	2
	16 ENGLAND 5	ADELAIDE	9	26	12.5	2	49	4
			-		14	3	69	4
	17 ENGLAND 6	MELBOURNE	9	12	6	2	17	1
			11	0	-			
1975	18 ENGLAND 1	BIRMINGHAM	10	3	15	8	15	5
			-		20	8	45	2
	19 ENGLAND 2	LORD'S	10	73	20	4	84	4
			-		33	10	80	1
	20 ENGLAND 3	LEEDS	10	11	28	12	53	1
			-		20	5	48	2
	21 ENGLAND 4	THE OVAL	10	28	19	7	44	2
					52	18	91	4
1975-76	22 WEST INDIES 1	BRISBANE	9	1	11	-	84	3
			-		16	3	72	3

			BATTING		BOWLING			
SEASON	MATCH	VENUE	NO	RUNS	OVERS	MAIDENS	RUNS	WICKETS
	23 WEST INDIES 2	PERTH	9 9	12 4	20 -	-	123	2
	24 WEST INDIES 3	MELBOURNE	9 -	25	14 15	2 1	56 70	4 3
	25 WEST INDIES 5	ADELAIDE	11 -	16	10 14	- -	68 64	2 2
	26 WEST INDIES 6	MELBOURNE	11 -	19	11.3 18	- 1	63 112	5 3
1976-77	27 PAKISTAN 1	ADELAIDE	10 -	0	19 47.7	1 10	104 163	1 5
	28 PAKISTAN 2	MELBOURNE	- 9	6	23 14	4 1	82 53	6 4
	29 PAKISTAN 3	SYDNEY	10 10	14 27	22.3 4	- -	114 24	3 2
1976-77	30 NEW ZEALAND 1	CHRISTCHURCH	10 -	19	31.2 18	6 1	119 70	2 2
	31 NEW ZEALAND 2	AUCKLAND	10 -	23	17.3 15.7	4 2	51 72	5 6
1976-77	32 ENGLAND CENTENARY TEST	MELBOURNE	10 9	10 25	13.3 34.4	2 7	26 139	6 5
1979-80	33 WEST INDIES 1	BRISBANE	9 -	0	29.1 2	8 -	104 3	4 -
	34 ENGLAND 1	PERTH	9 9	18 19	28 23	11 5	73 74	4 2
	35 WEST INDIES 2	MELBOURNE	8 8	12 0	36 3	7 -	96 9	3 -
	36 ENGLAND 2	SYDNEY	8 -	5	13.3 24.3	4 6	40 63	4 2
	37 WEST INDIES 3	ADELAIDE	8 8	16 0	24 26	3 6	78 75	5 -
	38 ENGLAND 3	MELBOURNE	8 -	8	33.1 33	9 6	60 78	6 5
1979-80	39 PAKISTAN 1	KARACHI	10 10	12 5	28 11	4 2	76 22	- -
	40 PAKISTAN 2	FAISALABAD	10 -	0	21 -	4	91	-
	41 PAKISTAN 3	LAHORE	- 10	1	42 -	9	114	3
1980	42 ENGLAND CENTENARY TEST	LORD'S	- -		15 19	4 5	43 53	4 1
1980-81	43 NEW ZEALAND 1	BRISBANE	8 -	24	18 15	7 1	36 53	2 6
	44 NEW ZEALAND 2	PERTH	8 -	8	23.5 15.1	5 7	63 14	5 2
	45 NEW ZEALAND 3	MELBOURNE	8 8	27 8	21 13	4 3	49 30	- 1
1980-81	46 INDIA 1	SYDNEY	8 -	5	20.2 18	3 2	86 79	4 3

SEASON	MATCH	VENUE	BATTING		BOWLING			
			NO	RUNS	OVERS	MAIDENS	RUNS	WICKETS
	47 INDIA 2	ADELAIDE	9	2	34	10	80	4
			9	10	19	7	38	2
	48 INDIA 3	MELBOURNE	9	19	25	6	65	4
			9	4	32.1	5	104	4
1981	49 ENGLAND 1	NOTTINGHAM	9	12	13	3	34	3
			-		16.4	2	46	5
	50 ENGLAND 2	LORD'S	10	40	35.4	7	102	-
			-		26.4	8	82	3
	51 ENGLAND 3	LEEDS	10	3	18.5	7	49	4
			10	17	25	6	94	3
	52 ENGLAND 4	BIRMINGHAM	9	18	18	4	61	2
			9	3	26	9	51	2
	53 ENGLAND 5	MANCHESTER	9	13	24.1	8	55	4
			9	28	46	13	137	2
	54 ENGLAND 6	THE OVAL	9	11	31.4	4	89	7
			9	8	30	10	70	4
1981-82	55 PAKISTAN 1	PERTH	9	16	9	3	18	5
			9	4	20	3	78	1
	56 PAKISTAN 2	BRISBANE	9	14	20	3	81	5
			-		19	4	51	4
	57 PAKISTAN 3	MELBOURNE	9	1	36.3	9	104	-
			9	4	-			
1981-82	58 WEST INDIES 1	MELBOURNE	9	1	26.3	3	83	7
			9	0	27.1	8	44	3
	59 WEST INDIES 2	SYDNEY	10	4	39	6	119	4
			-		20	6	50	2
	60 WEST INDIES 3	ADELAIDE	9	2	4.5	3	4	-
			9	1	4	-	17	-
1981-82	61 NEW ZEALAND 1	WELLINGTON	-		15	5	32	-
			-		-			
	62 NEW ZEALAND 2	AUCKLAND	10	9	39	7	106	3
			10	5	13	5	32	1
	63 NEW ZEALAND 3	CHRISTCHURCH	10	7	12	6	13	3
			-		-			
1982-83	64 ENGLAND 1	PERTH	10	2	38	13	96	3
			-		33	12	89	1
1982-83	65 SRI LANKA	KANDY	-		19	3	67	2
			-		11	3	40	1
1983-84	66 PAKISTAN 1	PERTH	9	0	13	3	26	1
			-		29	6	56	-
	67 PAKISTAN 2	BRISBANE	-		8	1	33	-
			-		2	-	10	-
	68 PAKISTAN 3	ADELAIDE	10	25	50.2	8	171	6
			10	4	-			
	69 PAKISTAN 4	MELBOURNE	11	2	38	11	113	2
			-		29	7	71	3
	70 PAKISTAN 5	SYDNEY	-		31.2	10	65	4
			-		29.5	5	88	4

IMAGE CREDITS

All other images are from Dennis Lillee's private collection.